The Eucharist and the Rosary

MYSTERY
MEDITATION
POWER
PRAYER

Matt Swaim

Liguori

ONE LIGUORI DRIVE
LIGUORI MO 63057-9999

Published by Liguori Publications
Liguori, Missouri
To order, call 800-325-9521
www.liguori.org

Imprimi Potest:
Thomas D. Picton, C.Ss.R.
Provincial, Denver Province
The Redemptorists

Imprimatur:
Most Reverend Robert J. Hermann
Auxiliary Bishop, Archdiocese of St. Louis

Library of Congress Cataloging-in-Publication Data

Swaim, Matt.
   The Eucharist and the Rosary : mystery, meditation, power, prayer / Matt Swaim.
—1st ed.
      p. cm.
   ISBN 978-0-7648-1873-8
   1. Mass—Meditations. 2. Mysteries of the Rosary. I. Title.
   BX2230.3.S82 2010
   264'.02036—dc22

                                                                    2009048743

Additional copyright acknowledgments are in Sources, page 117.

Liguori Publications, a nonprofit corporation, is an apostolate of the Redemptorists. To learn more about the Redemptorists, visit Redemptorists.com.

Printed in the United States of America
14 13 12 11 10   5 4 3 2

Contents

To Dan Egan for his keen observations, Greg Westwood for just the right amount of suggestions and reservations, and Brian Patrick and Anna Mitchell for their inexplicable and greatly appreciated patience.

Also, to my wife, Colleen, who made possible many otherwise impossible writing occasions.

Introduction

Roughly a year before I entered the Catholic Church at the Easter Vigil of 2005, I stopped looking at the rosary as an idolatrous talisman and started to look at it as a possible tool for contemplation. To say that in my pre-Catholic life I was a Gnostic would be going too far, but it would certainly be fair to describe my view of reality as emphasizing the spiritual and marginalizing the material. Essentially, even though I wasn't Catholic, I'd been objectifying the rosary and other material prayer aids for twenty-four years. I perceived the Catholic use of the rosary as akin to the way superstitious wart-washers bathed their blemishes in the moonlight. To me, the rosary was a religious security blanket, a placebo, something that Catholics clasped in antiquated piety to ward off whatever spiritual troubles might be assailing them at the time. In my mind, it was the Catholic version of a lucky rabbit's foot. No real power could be ascribed to it, but it could make its wielder feel as though he or she had temporary power over the circumstances of the moment.

Part of my reason for thinking about the rosary in this way had to do with a misunderstanding on my part as to what the rosary actually is. I thought the rosary was a set of beads arranged in a circular pattern with a dangling crucifix at the end. To me, the rosary was a trinket. It was what Catholics carried around instead of "WWJD" bracelets. Now I understand that the beads themselves are not the rosary, but rather something for one to hold while one prays the rosary. The rosary, I eventually came to understand, is not a device but a form of prayer.

Father Patrick Peyton, the "rosary priest," once said that if we were to somehow lose all of the Gospels, the narrative core of them would remain preserved in the rosary. This is the same rosary that was referred to by Padre Pio as a "weapon" and is regularly employed by countless Catholics in the battle against abortion, war, and other grave social evils. The structure of the rosary is simple enough that it can be learned by an elementary student, and yet the mysteries with which it connects us can outstretch the imaginational limits of the most theologically astute.

Frequent praying of the rosary immerses us in the Gospel story and causes us to see echoes of the Gospel in many different aspects of our lives. A seasoned devotee of the rosary can remember the Sorrowful Mystery of the Death of our Lord every time he or she sees a crucifix, or can perhaps call to mind specific pieces of art that correspond to each individual mystery during prayer. In this way, the rosary, which is shared by the universal Church, can also be a prayer that is capable of being personalized.

One might even say, with credibility, that individual Catholics have their own ways of "riffing" on the rosary. Some use the three Hail Marys that precede the recitation of the mysteries as an opportunity to pray for an increase in the theological virtues of faith, hope, and love. Others may offer the rosary for the intentions of the Holy Father, or perhaps pause to invoke the help of Saint Michael the Archangel at the close of the prayer. The possibilities for personalizing the rosary while remaining within its universality are seemingly endless.

In this limited volume, my hope is to reflect on one particular method of "riffing" on the rosary, namely, connecting the various elements of our experience of the Mass with the specific mysteries that we remember in this time-honored prayer of the Church.

The Mass itself is designed to communicate the core of the Gospel. This is also a function of the prayers of the rosary. And while there is no official declaration from the Church connecting the mysteries of the rosary with the elements of the Mass, from a popular devotional standpoint, it is certainly possible to see many aspects of the life of Christ that are common to both the rosary and the Mass.

As such, this is a work of personal devotion rather than liturgical exploration or even theological speculation. My hope is that the readers of this work will be able to see the wisdom of salvation history from an angle that they perhaps have not yet explored— namely that of viewing the Mass through the lens of the rosary and vice versa—as well as to take a fresh look at the ways in which we experience both of these prayers. Being Catholic means immersing ourselves in the Gospel. Hopefully, this small volume will serve to further immerse the reader in the mysteries of Scripture and Tradition that comprise our great faith.

MATT SWAIM

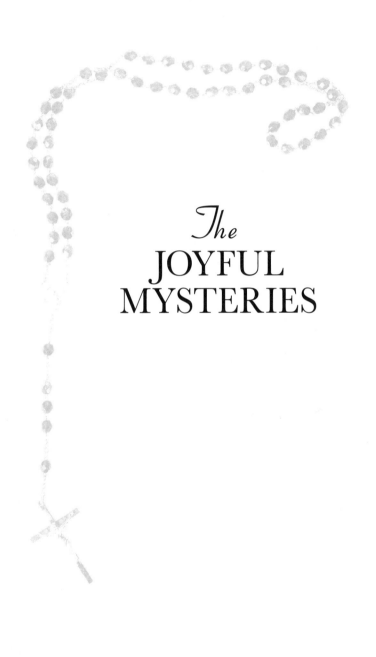

The
JOYFUL
MYSTERIES

The Annunciation

. . . .

"ONLY SAY THE WORD..."

✝ The first reception of the "Good News" or "Gospel" of Jesus Christ came not to a prominent religious leader, nor to an established prophet or scribe, but rather to a Jewish peasant girl, Mary of Nazareth. Her response to this mystery was not only that of faith in the truth of the message being presented, namely that she would be the mother of the Christ; it also reflected a spirit of obedience. Faith and works found their intersection at the moment of the announcement of Jesus' conception in the form of Mary's response to Gabriel, "Let it be with me according to your word" (Luke 1:38). Her statement of belief was a promise of action; she would personally care for the Messiah at his most vulnerable stage. These spoken words from God marked the entry point into history of the Incarnate Word of God.

The spoken and written word is the primary way in which we communicate. Jesus, the Word Himself, is therefore God's greatest communication to humanity. In the case of Mary's reception of the Gospel, the Word was not merely a message or abstract principle but Someone Incarnate. He took form inside of her, developed, matured, and became accessible to those outside of Mary, even though she initially received him in privacy. In the same way, when we hear the Gospel announced to us at every Mass, we should be attentive, responsive, and willing to allow the Word of the Lord to implant himself in us, to grow, and to mature to the point of making us able to share him with others. And in taking the Eucharist into our bodies, as Mary took Jesus into her womb, what is for us an intensely intimate moment of receiving Holy Communion becomes a potential avenue of grace for the world.

When we talk about Mary as the model for Christian life, we must begin by focusing on this pinpoint of Christian history; that there was a nanosecond in time where the Creator of the universe took on embryonic human flesh in the womb of a virgin, and that the hinge upon which all history swings is the annunciation. Kingdoms have risen and fallen based on what happened in this brief conversation between Mary and Gabriel.

As in the case of the parable of the sower in Matthew 13, the soil is a factor when it comes to projecting the harvest. When we hear the Gospel announced at Mass, we must, like Mary, remain fertile and receptive to what we are witnessing, because the Word of the Lord is a sown seed, a tangible investment that God makes in us through the person of his Son. It is our job to present ourselves as an environment in which the spoken word can manifest itself as the lived Word, by modeling ourselves after Mary, the immaculate template for all Christians.

From the very beginning of the Mass, we are guided by way of the *Kyrie Eleison* to recognize that any interaction between the human and the Divine is dependent upon God's mercy. In Moses' encounter with God atop Mount Sinai after the deliverance of the children of Israel from the hand of Pharaoh, the overwhelming superiority of "I AM" to human understanding meant that at best, Moses could only view God from behind so as not to be instantly immolated by the heat and light of YHWH's divine glory. Thus, at Mass, we are compelled to confess our sins and ask for mercy from the Font of Mercy himself before the liturgy can even move forward. In the same way, Mary, as is reported in Luke's Gospel, recognized an extension of mercy from the angel Gabriel on behalf of God when he spoke of the grace with which she had been filled in preparation for that moment. Her response was one of awe and bewilderment, such that Gabriel had to ask her to dismiss her fear.

How often do we approach Holy Communion with an attitude like Mary's, asking, "How can this be?" Have we ever tiptoed toward a eucharistic minister in such a way that he or she felt compelled to tell us not to be afraid before we received the Body of Christ into our persons? How often do we realize that we are selected from among all the peoples of the earth to welcome the Son of God sacramentally into our own bodies? It is a privilege that can be granted by mercy alone and not by our own achievements.

The word "annunciation" is derived from the same Latin root as the word "announcement," and the Liturgy of the Word, our prelude to the consecration of the elements of bread and wine, is all about announcement. Before we hear the designated readings for Mass, we sing the Gloria, which begins with the words of the angels to the shepherds in rural Bethlehem: "Glory to God in the highest, and peace to his people on Earth." These words alerted the shepherds to the fact that God had become man and that he would be taking his first physical breaths mere miles from the ground on which they stood. In our case, when we attend Mass, we must attune ourselves to the fact that Christ

“Most of society sees us as 'lost' or not worthy of their time and especially money, but by your generosity and willingness to assist us in our spiritual journey, you show us that you see us as Jesus truly does—as wayward sheep who lost our way, and who are in need of assistance to guide us back to the flock. For this we are truly grateful.**”**

John

“I read an old book of *Give Us This Day*. I really enjoyed it. . . . I really see the world differently than I did before. This was a gift that I needed.**”**

Trayce

“The structure of the morning and evening prayer found in this resource has encouraged my continual prayer all through-out the day. I have also enjoyed the meditations, reflections on the Saints and other various articles. Simple words may not convey my appreciation; still a thank you is definitely in order.**”**

Joseph

“The men have used the publication daily and ask me the middle each month if I have received the next month's issue and when ll they be receiving it? In short. . .they just love it and it is ving a tremendous impact on their spiritual well-being.**”**

Chaplain Jim

Share
HOPE

"I was in prison and you visited me." Matt 25:36

Share the blessing of

Give Us ThisDay®

Put *Give Us This Day* in the
hands of the incarcerated.
Working closely with prison
chaplains and ministers,
and with your support, we
provide thousands of copies to
correctional facilities throughout
the United States each month.

We can't do it without you.

Your generosity provides

FREE subscriptions to prisoners.

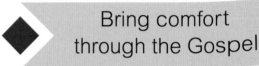

Bring comfort
through the Gospel

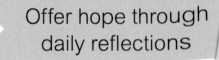

Offer hope through
daily reflections

Connect lives
through daily praye[r]

Learn more and donate at **GUTD.net/prison**

will become truly present under the appearance of bread and wine mere feet from where we sit in our pews.

The psalms that we hear, and to which we respond, are from the same set of Scriptures that the children of Israel would have used in their own religious tradition to communicate with God. Saint Athanasius once wrote that the bulk of the Scriptures speak *to* us, while the psalms speak *for* us. In the same way, Mary speaks *for* us, when she asks Gabriel, "How can this be?" (Luke 1:34). We ask that very question in the liturgy every time we intend to receive Christ, truly present in the Eucharist. We proclaim our own unworthiness to receive him and acknowledge that it is only the willingness of the Lord to declare us worthy that makes any of our participation in this Sacrament possible.

In Mary's case and ours, our indebtedness to The Word is a key aspect of the transaction. She asks that the conception of the Messiah take place according to the word of Gabriel the Archangel; in our situation, we ask that our preparation for reception of Communion be completed by the declaration of Christ, as did the centurion in Matthew 8: "…only say the word, and my soul shall be healed." Mary, more worthy than any of us, again serves as a model when it comes to requesting the fortitude to prepare ourselves to receive Christ into our very bodies.

Finally, we can see strong parallels between Incarnation and consecration. At a specific moment in history, the Word of God became flesh and blood. Likewise, at a specific moment in the Mass, bread and wine become flesh and blood. Mary was unable to fully verify with her senses the truth of what had occurred in her; in the same way, our senses alone fail us when it comes to recognizing Jesus in the Eucharist. But with Mary, we give our assent that truth transcends our senses. We acknowledge that truth is not dependent upon our ability to perceive it. And in this case, the truth is that the annunciation makes Christ present in Mary, just as the consecration of the elements of Communion make Christ present upon the altar.

When Mary received the Incarnate Word into her womb, she responded with gratitude and praise. Our goal should be to do the same, living out the response with which we conclude the end of each Mass: "Thanks be to God!"

REFLECTION QUESTIONS

❶ How can I say "yes" to God in such a way that the Word can become incarnate in my own life?

❷ Am I aware of my own unworthiness to receive the sacraments? Am I aware of the grace that is available to cover my unworthiness and that invites me to participate in the sacraments?

❸ Do I take for granted my own gift of baptism? Like Mary, do I respond to God's desire to dwell in me with appropriate wonder?

The Visitation

· · · · · · · · · · · · · · · · ·

"HOW CAN THIS BE?"

✝ Connected with Mary's sense of unworthiness is her cousin Elizabeth's incredulity at the notion that God could possibly be physically present in the womb of her relative, and further, that this Messiah *in utero* would be arriving on her doorstep. However, Elizabeth's exclamation of *dis*belief should not be read as one of *un*belief. Elizabeth's response to the arrival of Mary, "And why has this happened to me, that the mother of my Lord comes to me?" (Luke 1:43), is reflective of King David's reaction in 2 Samuel 6:9, as the Ark of the Covenant makes its way to Jerusalem: "How can the ark of the Lord come into my care?" Both David and Elizabeth were able to recognize the presence of God in the situation without requiring any explanation as to what and whom they were welcoming. David knew that the Ark carried things worthy of reverence, even gravity: heavenly manna, the Law, and the priestly rod of Aaron. In visiting Elizabeth, Mary bore within her womb the New Manna, the fulfillment of the Law himself, and the initiator of the Christian priesthood. In the case of both David and Elizabeth, humility was the first response. Humility should be our first response as well as we approach the sacrament of the altar.

A Catholic pastor friend of mine once shared with me a conversation between him and an evangelical minister. The minister remarked that if he were to believe what we Catholics believe (namely that Christ is truly present in the Eucharist), then he would feel compelled to crawl to the altar on his hands and knees out of reverence to receive Communion. How casually do we who believe approach the supreme privilege of receiving the Body and Blood of Jesus, who is for us the difference between heaven and hell?

Also implicit in the story of Mary visiting Elizabeth is the idea of pilgrimage. When we attend Mass, we aren't often making the long and arduous trek, as Mary did, to the "hill country." More likely than not, our Church lies within the confines of our respective zip codes. However, there is an aspect of pilgrimage that is often overlooked when we travel from what the Second Vatican Council calls the "domestic Church" (namely our homes and families) to the Church proper.

When we understand our own "visitation" to our Church of membership, do we see it as a mere obligation, or do we enter into it as a trip from our particular house on a particular street toward a portal between the eternal and the temporal? It's easy to think of a drive (or walk) to Mass as a Sunday or weekday routine where we all show up in the same place with a common destination, like airplane or bus passengers, and once it's over, we move on as though we were never attached to our fellow travelers by anything more than the formality of seating choice. What if we understood the Mass properly, as a foreshadowing of our ultimate destination, namely, heaven? Would we perhaps be more appreciative of the sacrament that was confected upon our altars and reposed within our tabernacles? Reflecting upon the Mass in this way would help us develop our thinking about this journey more in terms of pilgrimage than obligation.

Elizabeth's respect for the one who brings her the Messiah is also a point of interest. In the case of the Liturgy of the Eucharist, the one who carries Christ to us is the priest, who is himself an *alter Christus,* another Christ. One theological mistake often made by non-Catholic Christians is that of treating Mary as a mere container that God used for the purpose of incubating his Son and then callously discarded. This parallels a mistake we sometimes make in the Catholic Church, one of treating the priests whose consecrated hands make Christ present on the altar as mere sacramental vending machines. If the office of the priesthood is what we say it is, namely, the ambassadorial effort of Christ to intimately connect with his people, then we ought to treat those called to that role with the greatest reverence possible for a human vocation.

The reason that the response of Elizabeth to the Christ-carrying Mary is striking to us is because our own response to our Christ-carrying priests is usually underwhelming by comparison. Many of us, when we we receive Communion, routinely cross ourselves and head back to our pews mechanically. Elizabeth's exultant response when she meets our Lord is significant. Her response becomes even more startling when we understand that Elizabeth has only one recorded interaction with Jesus in the Gospels, and this before he even exits Mary's womb. Aside from the implications this episode has for a Catholic reverence for unborn life, there are major devotional implications as well. In the Catholic Church, through the mystery of the Eucharist, we daily have opportunities to receive Christ into our bodies. According to Luke's account, it would not be unlikely for Elizabeth to go six months without seeing her cousin. Perhaps this added to her appreciation of the event, but it also highlights our own occasional lack of appreciation for the Mass.

Elizabeth rejoiced once she came within shouting distance of our unborn Lord. At Mass, do we begin our internal rejoicing once we realize that we are in proximity of the Word made flesh? Are we seized with a thrill when we see the spires of the church on the horizon? Do we wait until we've actually received him to rejoice? Or are we utterly oblivious, receiving Communion because everyone else is or because we're with our families, or because, even though we know we shouldn't receive, we just don't want our fellow parishioners to trip over us as they make their way down the aisles?

Elizabeth's response to Mary's visitation should inform every encounter we have with Christ in the Eucharist; we should rejoice with her at the way in which the Word made flesh has made himself available to us.

The embryonic John the Baptist jumps at the arrival of Jesus. I myself have the liturgical sense to note that I don't think it's the best idea for us to be bounding down the aisles after receiving Communion. But how often do we receive Christ as though we were being handed a pound of ham at the deli or redeeming a parking voucher? This encounter between heaven and earth is unlike any other transaction in which we participate in our everyday lives. It is self encountering the Divine in the most profound sense available to our human understanding.

REFLECTION QUESTIONS

❶ Do I approach the sacraments with the appropriate level of humility, untainted by either flippancy or scrupulousness?

❷ Do I view my attendance at Mass as mere obligation or as an opportunity for pilgrimage?

❸ Do I treat my pastor with the reverence due someone who carries Christ to me, or do I treat him like a sacramental cashier?

The Nativity

· ·
"LET US GO TO BETHLEHEM."

✝ Perhaps the best place to start when it comes to seeing the Nativity in the context of the Mass is to look at another "annunciation," that of the angels to the shepherds, who were awed to be among those appointed to witness the entrance of the Messiah into the material world as a material being.

The shepherds were the commoners, the "blue-collar" workers of first-century Palestine. Shepherding was the first job of many children in the days before lawnmowers. If it were an option in today's culture, parents might make their teenage sons herd sheep over the summer in order to make them think more seriously about higher education. Shepherds smelled as bad as anyone who worked alongside animals could be expected to smell, and keeping close company with a shepherd was not exactly something one would readily volunteer to do at the end of a work day.

And yet, the shepherds were selected. Not the religious leaders, nor the tax collectors, nor the government officials. In a shocking first indicator of the upside-down kingdom that Jesus would establish, the lowly minimum wage earners of Bethlehem were elevated to the position of firsthand witnesses of the hinge-point of all history. A similar sentiment could be offered about us when we drag our sorry working bones to Mass. Who are we, but the people who have been elevated out of our nagging and laborious routines to an audience with the Almighty?

Such was the case with the shepherds. From the fields they came, out of their ordinary routine and into a moment of eternal significance. This opportunity to connect with something beyond ourselves, outside of our day-to-day lives, is the very thing that is offered to us whenever we choose to darken the doors of our churches and become present to the Christ who makes himself present to us at the consecration of bread and wine.

At the other end of the spectrum lie the Magi. And while a critical perusal of the historical record reveals that they weren't exactly the first on the scene to welcome the birth of Christ, the fact of the matter is, they were on the guest list.

The work of the Magi was perhaps the opposite of manual labor. They held what we might see as the first-century equivalent of "desk jobs," in that thinking and writing was their stock and trade. They were paid to analyze facts and figures, much like those who spend their days within the confines of cubicle farms, trying to make sense of the words and numbers that cross their desks in mind-numbing fashion. At some point these Magi, who studied the mathematical and logical patterns of the stars, found something that they did not anticipate. They found an anomaly on their astronomical spreadsheet. A star had appeared where a star was not supposed to be. And so, like the blue-collar shepherds, the white-collar Magi were also summoned to witness the most critical event in all of human history.

There was angelic presence at the Incarnation, as evidenced by Gabriel's message to Mary. But the angels were also present at the Nativity of Christ, the full realization of the advent of the Messiah. The angels are also present at every Mass, when the presence of Jesus is recognized by all in attendance, as his flesh and blood overtake the man-made gifts of bread and wine. The priest even vocalizes this prayer as an acknowledgement of the intersection of heaven and earth when he leads us in the *Sanctus,* the same prayer that angels and elders are seen praying before the throne of God in the book of Revelation.

The priestly celebrant makes reference to the presence of the angels at every Mass. The liturgy prescribes that he recognize the fact that Mary, the Virgin Mother of God, and all the angels and saints join us in the hymn to Christ present on the altar. A similar scene takes place in the stable of Bethlehem. As such, we sing as a congregation that God is "Holy," three times over.

In the idiom of Scripture, when something is repeated three times, it means that the statement in question is being reinforced in the superlative form. In our own language, it might be helpful to think of the first "holy" as corresponding to "good," the second to "better," and the third to "best." The angels, who are pure spirit in their makeup, recognize the spirit of God in the sacrament as they did in Bethlehem, and we echo their recognition of this presence at the consecration of the elements. When Christ became present in history, angels bore witness. When Christ becomes present upon the altar, angels bear witness as well.

The Mass of Christ can be a strange event for Catholics, as well as for all Christian congregations who choose to make liturgical observation of the birth of Jesus. At few other Church services are we as confronted with such a diverse sea of human-ity. Some of these irregular attendees come to Church out of a desire to please more pious family members. Some may come independent of any family at all, seeing Christmas as a chance to possibly dip their toes in the waters of religion in a setting where they might be most likely to remain anonymous. Others may have little religious impulse at all, but feel drawn to unbury the mystery of Christmas from the excessive materialistic garbage that has been piled atop it.

I wonder what each of the groups who greeted the baby Jesus must have thought of one another and themselves—they must have been at least a little confused at the kind of company this newborn King intended on keeping. Were the shepherds self-conscious of their smell? Were the late-arriving Magi embarrassed that they hadn't shown up earlier? Were all involved parties speculating as to why Mary and Joseph didn't seem to have any of the rest of their family present to help welcome the Christ child into the world?

We have no official knowledge of what either the shepherds or wise men did with their lives after their encounter with the Messiah at his earliest stages of life. In the same way, we may never know in this life what takes place in the souls of those who come to Church on December 25 and perhaps are never seen again within the walls of our parish afterward. We might be tempted to guess at whether the guests we are surrounded by at midnight Mass are local or have made pilgrimage from afar. But we cannot deny that there is something about the Christ child that inexplicably draws people from all walks of life to recognize God in a setting that makes all of us in one sense strange to one another but, at the same time, unified in our wonder at what happened in Bethlehem at the first Christmas.

As the priest prepares to consecrate the bread and wine into the Body and Blood of Jesus, he utters this prayer: "By the mystery of this water and wine, may we come to share in the divinity of Christ, who humbled himself to share in our humanity." This is the aim and final end of Catholic eschatology; because Christ was born a sinless man, we have the opportunity as humans to be cleansed from our sins to share in heavenly eternity with him. On this premise lies our means of achieving heaven. The Incarnation affirms God's eternal investment in a common ground between the material and the spiritual, that we who are a union of body and soul here on Earth can have a share in eternity at the resurrection, invited to join divinity in heaven as resurrected unions of body and soul.

REFLECTION QUESTIONS

❶ With which group of people invited to witness the birth of the Lord do I most closely relate?

❷ How does the assortment of those present at the Nativity help me to better appreciate the assortment of people with whom I gather at Mass?

❸ In what ways does the Advent of Christ in Bethlehem help me understand his coming to be with us in the Eucharist?

The Presentation at the Temple

· ·
"LOOKING FOR THE REDEMPTION"

✝ Jesus was presented at the Temple with a sacrifice of ritual purity on the eighth day, in accordance with the Mosaic law. This was not a sacrifice intended to forgive the sins of either Jesus or Mary (of which we know there were none), but was offered to fulfill the ritual obligations required of all Jews after the birth of a firstborn child. As we approach the Mass, in preparation for receiving holy Communion, we are called to cleanse ourselves as well or else refrain from receiving the sacrament. And while mortal sin is certainly a non-negotiable reason to abstain from receiving in the Eucharist, there are other reasons of a more ritual nature for which we are asked to excuse ourselves from Communion, and they are neither arbitrary nor without logical purpose.

Ritually speaking, we are asked to fast an hour before Mass, not because God has created a random hoop for us to jump through, but because he wants us to ready our appetites for the bread that came down from heaven, namely Jesus in the Eucharist. Likewise, we are told that we must be in the proper disposition in order to receive Communion. Merely "showing up" does not constitute the kind of "active participation" encouraged by the Second Vatican Council. In his apostolic exhortation, *Sacramentum Caritatis,* Pope Benedict XVI reminds us that *true* "active participation" at Mass doesn't mean singing in the choir or serving as an usher, honorable as these contributions on our part may be. At its core, he reminds us that active participation consists of working toward a "greater awareness of the mystery being celebrated [at Mass] and its relationship to daily life."

We can look at the sacrifice of the Holy Family as a model of active participation. Mary and Joseph did not present their sacrifices at the Temple simply because that was what one did as a Jew, or just because they wanted to remain in good social standing in the community, but because they wanted to honor God by whatever means God had prescribed for them. So often, we demand that God be honored on our terms rather than his. Even some of our modern Catholic hymn texts reflect this— sometimes at Mass, we end up singing about how wonderful we are and lapse into thinking that Mass is about us rather than about something bigger than us. However, all this kind of mentality displays is either laziness or lack of humility on our part; it means that consciously or subconsciously, we have fallen into the trap of thinking that the God who made an uncountable number of galaxies should suspend his pre-eminence each Sunday morning so as to accommodate our stomachs or our wandering thoughts. And while Jesus in the Incarnation condescended to us, it was not to bring God downward, but to bring us upward. Fortunately, Mary and Joseph lacked no such kind of humility, as we learn from Luke's account of the presentation of Jesus at the Temple; they offered the Messiah to God because they knew he was given to them out of trust and not entitlement.

As in the case of Elizabeth, the examples of Simeon and Anna help us when it comes to understanding the expectancy with which we should approach the Eucharist. These two aged holy persons had waited a lifetime to come into personal contact with the Messiah; in our cases, we have the privilege of receiving him on a daily basis through the frequent availability of Mass. Luke, whose Gospel records Mary's *Magnificat,* also records Simeon's hymn of praise *(Nunc Dimittis)*, wherein he proclaims a sense of final peace at being allowed to encounter Jesus. Do we have a sense of an ultimate, intimate meeting with God when we receive the Eucharist, or do we treat our reception of Communion as obligatory, a cold and legal fulfillment of a precept?

Simeon and Anna met Christ in a sacred setting, namely the Temple. Like them, we encounter God in many general ways as we go about our daily activities; in the stranger, in our loved ones, in the poor. However, there has been ordained for us a particular sacred setting in which to encounter Jesus, namely the Mass, in the re-established Temple of our Catholic Churches, realized in the tabernacles of each individual sanctuary.

The Mass itself is a sacrifice. Mary and Joseph came to offer something in exchange for something. Sacrifice is the way in which we make our appeal to God. As Saint John Vianney has written, "where there is no more sacrifice, there is no more religion." We will never appreciate that for which we have offered nothing in order to receive. The Mass, while it can be viewed as a meal, is first a sacrifice. It is us presenting that which we have, receiving what God has to give us in return, and then offering that gift *from* God back *to* God. As one friend has put it, "If you want a meal with friends, go to McDonald's. If you want a foretaste of heaven, go to Mass." Many non-Catholic Christian communities see Communion as an opportunity to memorialize Christ's death and solidify a shared experience. There is value and validity in this, but in Catholicism, we are taken beyond that, carried into the one sacrifice extended through all eternity, and we consume the Paschal Lamb of God as an act of full participation in the mysterious sacrifice of the Eucharist. Mary and Joseph understood the importance of offering something to God that was originally given to them by God. We offer to God our desire to know him more deeply, which is itself a gift from God.

Finally, the purification which Mary sought through her presentation of Jesus at the Temple is something that we ourselves revisit every time we go to Mass. If we are correctly oriented, we acknowledge that we do not approach God as we approach one another. If light has no fellowship with darkness, we must banish the darkness within us if we dare to approach the light. As we enter our churches, we acknowledge this by blessing ourselves with holy water and the Sign of the Cross. Furthermore, the penitential rite at the beginning of Mass allows us to recall and repent of our sins. When we participate in these actions, we express our belief that first of all, sin exists, and that second of all, we have been in fellowship with it. Light can only have fellowship with light, and it is that fellowship which we seek. In Mary's case, she did not seek purification because of her sin, but because she understood that the purer the vessel, the more ready it could be to receive all that the Lord had to offer.

REFLECTION QUESTIONS

❶ Do I understand the necessity of making myself a holy communicant before receiving holy Communion?

❷ When I approach the Mass, do I insist that God be available to me on my terms, or do I have the humility to approach him on his terms?

❸ As I approach Communion, what are those things which most often need to be purified from me in order to allow the grace of receiving the Eucharist to manifest itself most perfectly?

The
Finding in the Temple
. . . .
"DID YOU NOT KNOW THAT I MUST
BE IN MY FATHER'S HOUSE?"

✝ Matthew's account of the parable of the sheep and the goats in Chapter 25 of his Gospel shows us that Christ is present in the least among us. We know also through the tenth chapter of Saint Paul's first letter to the Corinthians that Christ is present in the community of believers. Seeing Jesus in the disadvantaged and in other believers are vitally important ways, as Christians, of looking at him. But there is a unique place and a unique way which our Lord has ordained for us to meet him here on earth that surpasses all other forms of encounter—through the participation in his sacramental Body and Blood in the Eucharist.

We understand that Christ's presence under the appearance of bread and wine is treated as the most important form of relationship with him because of the way we conduct ourselves when we approach holy Communion. Non-Catholic Christians have the opportunity to encounter Christ in the poor, and they have the opportunity to encounter Christ in other believers. But we reserve reception of the Eucharist to Catholics, because this is the most profound, intimate, and commitment-requiring manifestation of Christ's presence among us. The Eucharist, which we receive in our churches, demands that we gather at a certain time in a certain place and in a certain way to participate in this substantial presence of Jesus. It is no mere spiritual communion or fond memorial, but rather a personal encounter with the substantial presence of Christ under the appearance of bread and wine. He has humbled himself to meet with us on our terms; therefore, it is only fitting that we accept the terms he has set with humility.

The idea of the sanctity of a sanctuary takes on a different meaning in Catholic churches than in other Christian communities. Growing up as a Nazarene teenager in a central Ohio church, our "sanctuary," as it were, had no tabernacle and no consecrated hosts to put in one if we did have it. To complicate matters, in my junior high years, our church engaged in a building campaign with the honorable and well-intentioned approach of maximizing our space to accommodate both the spiritual and practical mission of the church. In both the old and new architectural plans, the "sanctuary" was so called not because it held the reposed Body and Blood of Jesus (as do Catholic sanctuaries), but because that was the room where we heard the preaching; it was where we were summoned by whoever was at the pulpit to deeper relationship with Jesus Christ. However, I remember (not so fondly) a perennial responsibility I spent many a post-Sunday night service trying to escape: each of the chairs used for Sunday morning worshipers had to be taken apart and stored by Monday so as to accommodate the middle-of-the-week basketball leagues, lock-ins, and a host of other events that the worship space was also designed to hold.

Despite my conversion to Catholicism only a few years ago, I hold no malice against this former church of mine, because I acknowledge that their theology and understanding of apostolic tradition was anything but sacramental in its nature. "Sanctuary," for that congregation, was more of a temporal architectural distinction than an integral theological distinction. In this kind of non-sacramental ecclesial theology, there could be no consecrated eucharistic Christ and therefore no tabernacle in which our Lord could be reposed. As a matter of fact, the room in which we worshipped on Sunday mornings had a couple of titles. Some called it the "sanctuary," while others called it the "all-purpose room." As a result, a person who walked at random into this section of the building might be as likely to encounter a dodge-ball tournament as a revival service.

In American Christianity, distaste for organized religion has led to the assertion, perhaps rightly so, that the Church is "not a building." However, this idea can be taken too far. The idea of a general notion of sacred space has validity—any place in which we can pray is a place that is, on some level, sacred. If we believe that God is the creator of heaven and earth, then we believe that his creation is "good," as he says repeatedly in the first chapter of Genesis. C. S. Lewis warned against the notion that an omnipresent God could be confined inside a building, writing that "all ground is holy, and every bush (could we but perceive it) [is] a Burning Bush."

And yet to assert that all ground is holy is not the same thing as saying that all ground is equally holy. When we expand the idea of sacred space so far that it comes to encompass all locations equally, we find not that all ground has become holier, but that the holiest of grounds have become less holy. And we know that despite his experience of the burning bush, there were certain places where Moses was allowed to wear shoes.

Some architects of the "megachurch" movement talk about the need to reduce "cognitive dissonance" between church and other aspects of our daily routines, such as our work, shopping, and home lives. Unfortunately, however, making the environmental disparity between church and the mall smaller is of great benefit to the malls, but isn't nearly as beneficial to the church. Catholics who have a proper eucharistic mindset understand this need to treat churches differently. Our voices soften as we enter the building. We remind ourselves of our baptism by blessing ourselves with holy water as we pass through the vestibule. And despite the amount of enthusiasm and attention we might devote to professional athletics, I must say, I've never seen someone genuflect toward home plate before taking his or her seat at a baseball game.

Many who gravitate toward the New Age movement also gravitate toward Thomas Merton, which has always confused me. I've walked in Merton's footsteps at the Abbey of Gethsemani, where he spent much of his life as a Trappist monk. I've stood in front of gnarled trees about which he wrote extensively with words of great spiritual clarity and mystical insight. I've marveled at how he was able to notice the handiwork and presence of God in the simplest aspects of nature. Others who would label themselves "spiritual" people have expressed similar wonder. I mention my confusion, because I haven't seen the same level of wonder from these admirers when they read about Merton's desire to become a priest. It begs an obvious question: if Merton could adequately encounter God through a walk in the woods, then why would he go through the trouble of something so formal and "religious" as ordination, unless it meant for him an even higher level of encounter with the Almighty? More than that, why even submit himself to the rigors of contemplative monasticism in the first place, unless that vocation provided for him a spiritual advantage worth renouncing everything to follow?

The spiritual crisis of our culture is that it is too focused on mere spirituality. God is everywhere, says our neo-Gnostic culture, and it ends up finding God nowhere. We are "spiritual" people, and not "religious" people, and so we are Godless people. What if we were to express to our spouses that we don't need to spend time with them or express our appreciation for them in formal terms, explaining to them that they are with us in spirit wherever we go?

We can and should expect to find Jesus in the needy and in our fellow believers. We feel the presence of God in his creation. But above and beyond that, Christ calls us back to the sacramental experience of him in the context of his Church as if to say, "Did you not know I would be in my Father's house?"

REFLECTION QUESTIONS

❶ How well do I understand the uniqueness of encountering Jesus in the Eucharist as compared to the other ways in which I meet him?

❷ How do I approach Mass differently than I approach other aspects of my life such as work, recreation, and meals?

❸ Am I more focused on the spiritual aspects of Communion than the material and substantial aspects, or vice versa? How can I better understand the Eucharist so to balance my perspective of what actually happens at Mass?

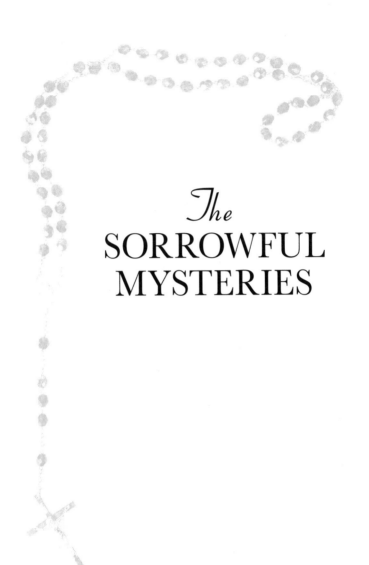

The
SORROWFUL
MYSTERIES

$\mathcal{T}he$
Agony in the Garden
· · · · · · · · · · · · · · · ·
"WATCH AND PRAY."

✝ At the beginning of the rite of consecration, we note in the liturgy that Jesus gave us his Body and Blood on "the night before he suffered." When someone is preparing for death, their priorities become clear. In the case of Jesus, his priority was to offer to his disciples the sacrament of the Eucharist and to commission them to carry on this same sacrifice, presenting it to others. As the Gospel accounts attest, Jesus left the Last Supper neither to assemble a coup nor to turn himself in to the Jewish or Roman authorities, but to pray in the garden of Gethsemane where he would wrestle in agony, God the Son with God the Father.

In recognition of the contents of the cup he was about to drink, Jesus expressed a briefly reluctant obedience. We perhaps express a reluctant obedience on certain Sunday mornings after late Saturday nights. Maybe that's because we prefer the comfort of our mattresses to the stark and unyielding wood of our pews and kneelers; maybe, like James and John in Mark 10, we don't understand what's in the cup; or maybe we *do* understand the implications of receiving the cup over which Jesus prayed and don't think we have the courage to do so. Whatever the case may be, this brief hesitation on the part of our Lord, which preceded his resolute obedience, should serve as a comfort to us.

As he entered the garden of Gethsemane to experience his agony, Jesus told Peter, James, and John to watch and pray. For the majority of the Mass, that is what we are doing—watching and praying as the priest in the person of Jesus prepares for sacrifice, just as Jesus himself prepared for his own bodily sacrifice when he prayed in the garden of Gethsemane. And watching and praying, while it might sound like an easy job, can be demanding. After a late Saturday night, we might be tempted to follow the example of the Apostles, who dozed off even as the sacrifice was being prepared. But watching and praying, according to the Church, is the most crucial part of the active participation at Mass to which we are all called.

How are we to watch? The view of Jesus was hidden from the sight of the Apostles. They were not so much called to watch Jesus himself as they were to watch *on behalf* of Jesus. It is not as though Jesus was unable to defend himself against the arresting party that had been assembled by Judas; Jesus' healing of Malchus' ear after it was severed by Peter shows us that he had complete control over the situation. Neither was Jesus calling the Apostles to watch on behalf of themselves so that they could run and hide at the sight of danger, even though that is what Peter and James ended up doing. They were to watch, unblinking, the plight of the Messiah, because they were the ones who had only hours before been ordained to proclaim his death until he came in glory. By witnessing his sacrifice, they were being called to participate in his sacrifice.

And how are we to pray? Certainly, we are called to do so in a more faithful manner than even the hand-picked Apostles of Jesus did, despite the fact that they were fortified by the daily earthly presence of our Lord, and we, by contrast, are fortified by his sacramental presence. Therefore, in order to learn how we must pray in the context of the mystery of Christ's agony in the garden, we must enter into his own tortured prayer, even though the most elite of his Apostles failed to do so. Jesus was appealing to Peter, James, and John to unify their prayer with his so that they would be strengthened to unify their sacrifice with his. The Apostles' falling asleep on the job meant that this admonition to pray was one of many requests made by Jesus that his followers, including us, would ignore in favor of our own comfort.

The petition of Jesus in the garden is a prayer that we are at least in part able to fulfill by our participation in holy Communion. He prays in earnest that the Church be one. Saint Paul picks up on this in his first letter to the Corinthians, when he reminds us that we all partake in the one loaf as one body, moving us toward the oneness in which Jesus prayed we would all remain as he sweated blood in Gethsemane.

Unfortunately, there are many ways in which today's followers of Christ are not one. The most obvious indication of this is the number of independent and unaffiliated Christian communities that exist around the world. Some have split over the meaning of Communion; some over the meaning of baptism; some over points as trivial as whether or not guitars should be allowed in worship. And in these communities, the less commonality they share in liturgical matters, the less likely they are to be unified in theological and doctrinal matters. As the Latin idiom states, *Lex orandi, lex credendi* (The law of prayer is the law of belief). To say that prayer and belief can exist independently of one another requires quite the suspension of *dis*belief.

As Catholics, we understand that there is a unity of the human person that corresponds to the unity of the Body of Christ. The closer we are to becoming one in our worship, the closer we come to understanding the oneness that Christ yearned for in his Church. The way we pray together is the way that we believe together, and that way of prayer has its fruit in the one loaf that we share as one body.

The model of Jesus dialoguing with the Father in the garden of Gethsemane gives us insight into how we can be one as the Body of Christ. Jesus prays that we be one as he and the Father are one, but even the Trinity doesn't run on autopilot. The very fact that Jesus has a conversation with the Father instead of mechanically accepting orders from the Father shows the presence of deeply critical thought within the mystery of the Trinity. And the Church is not afraid of dialogue, even if it may have a time-tested distaste for ideologues. Our model for conversation with the world is based on the method of God himself, who sent an ambassador to us in the form of his Son so as to more effectively engage the world in conversation but not compromise.

At Mass, what makes Catholics one is the common reception of the Eucharist. The same Jesus is presented to each person who processes toward the altar. And he is present, regardless of the age, weight, height, race, dress, or disposition of the recipient. Regardless even of our response, it is the same Christ whom we all receive.

Prior to the sacrifice of the cross, Jesus knew the importance of kneeling before the Father in prayer. As we gather in our pews, if we are to model the disposition of Christ before the re-presentation of his sacrifice, our focus should not be on the church bulletin, nor upon who looks ridiculous to us in a particular Sunday morning get-up, but on kneeling before the Father in earnest preparation.

During his agony in the garden, Jesus showed us how to pray when everything was on the line. If we are to model ourselves after him, we should be wrestling with our responsibility to make a worthy Communion, fighting to reclaim a worthy disposition, blocking out the temptation to turn either our bodies or souls away from the path set before us. And given the climates we may encounter as we kneel in our pews, it may be one of the most difficult spiritual disciplines to master as we prepare for the sacrifice of the Mass.

REFLECTION QUESTIONS

❶ How prayerfully do I approach Communion?

❷ What effort do I make to answer Jesus' prayer for oneness in his Church when I participate in the Eucharist?

❸ What distractions am I faced with as I prepare for Mass? How can I actively work to block out those distractions so as to "watch and pray" as Jesus instructed?

The
Scourging at the Pillar
·
"BY HIS BRUISES WE ARE HEALED."

✝ Those who are veterans at meditating upon the rosary
know how to call to mind visual images of each individual
mystery as it is being prayed. For me, the mental image I connect with the scourging of Jesus is perhaps the most vivid of
any other mystery because of having seen Mel Gibson's 2004
movie, *The Passion of the Christ.* The abject cruelty with which
our Lord was beaten at the pillory as portrayed in that film
is seared into my brain and comes back to mind every time I
reach this Sorrowful Mystery.

Having spent time in many non-Catholic Christian communities, I've been well exposed to the reasoning behind presenting a bare cross in place of a corpus-bearing crucifix. The
argument many Christians make for a Christ-less cross is that
we do not serve a crucified Lord but a risen one. And indeed,
as Catholics, we boldly proclaim that Christ has conquered
death. However, we cannot deny that death itself is ugly and
that no death is uglier than the death of Jesus.

Upon first seeing that violent image of the scourging of Jesus
in *The Passion,* I remember thinking to myself that out of all
of the sufferings of our Lord, this particular mystery was the
hardest for me to accept. Why portray something on film, or
in art of any kind, that was so brutally, mercilessly, and—to
many non-Catholic film reviewers—so unredemptively violent?

Couldn't it be possible to understand Christ's salvific sacrifice without seeing his flesh so lacerated by Roman torturers that even his rib-bones were exposed? Even the most visceral artistic works of medieval piety seemed to show more restraint.

The words of the Mass help us here. As the priest begins the words of consecration, he recounts the fact that the death of Christ was "a death he freely accepted." And understanding what was set before him in the garden of Gethsemane, we know that his free acceptance encompassed even this, the most brutal of his sufferings.

When I think of Jesus' scourging, I wince at the envisioned impact of every blow. It is the one mystery that connects me deeply enough with the physical pain of Christ to where I can get some small sense of the agonizing effect that my sin has on Jesus. And if, as Saint Paul writes, this knowledge of mine is imperfect, then how agonizingly perfected is the pain experienced by Jesus in his perfect knowledge every time he sees us straying from created goodness and racing to indulge our own concupiscience?

We often speak of ultimate sacrifice as the willingness to "take a bullet" for someone. I probably am not alone in my sentiment that taking a bullet for someone would be preferable to most other forms of sacrifice. It sounds much more appealing to me than being asked to drown for someone or be burned for someone. And so we rightly laud the sacrifice of saints such as Maximillian Kolbe, who was willing to starve for an innocent family man in a concentration camp, because we know that it's one thing to volunteer for a swift death on behalf of another and something else altogether to volunteer to bear torture on behalf of another. And yet this is exactly the sort of sacrifice to which Christ willingly subjected himself when he agreed not only to die for our sins, but also to be tortured for our sins.

In the book, *The Princess Bride,* as the villainous Prince Humperdinck prepares to square off with the heroic Westley, Humperdinck challenges Westley to a duel to the death. Westley responds in an unexpected manner—he challenges Humperdinck to duel "to the pain." When he describes the slow torture that this sort of duel would require, Humperdinck becomes significantly less enthusiastic about the prospect of a duel. As in the case of Prince Humperdinck, most of us would be more open to the prospect of martyrdom if we thought death would be instant.

Jesus, as we know from his agony in Gethsemane, saw the path laid before him, and knew his death would be anything but quick. And yet, he prayed that the Father's will be done, even has he saw ahead to the brutal scourging that he would receive at the hands of the Roman soldiers.

We refer to the sacrament of the Eucharist as an "unbloody sacrifice." And yet we know it is a re-presentation of a horribly bloody sacrifice, reminding us of the disfigured Jesus who accepted blow after blow from a jeering audience intent on making his death as long and torturous a process as possible. It's hard for us to envision the bloodiness of the original sacrifice when we see our eucharistic Lord elevated under the accidents of a pristine and seemingly bloodless wafer. Eastern Catholics who receive a host dipped in the reddened symbol of the transformed chalice perhaps have an easier time making the connection. But we must embrace the fact that in order to understand the circumstances which brought about our salvation, we must become more contemplatively involved in the "active participation" at Mass to which we are called as Catholics.

The inhuman scourging of Jesus is horrifying. Its depiction in *The Passion of the Christ* is one of the main reasons that the film received an R-rating. Even his crucifixion itself can at times be easier to stomach. Most of the crucifixes on display in our churches stop short of depicting in graphic detail the wounds Christ received at the hands of those who beat him. And yet the Church in her wisdom forces us to look directly at, even to meditate upon, the torn flesh of our Lord. And she has done so for two reasons: first, so that we can begin, however imperfectly, to understand the harm that our sin causes to Jesus; and second, so that we can get a glimpse of the kind of love he exhibited by freely accepting such an undeserved punishment.

REFLECTION QUESTIONS

❶ Do I realize the fact that my sin directly causes Christ's pain? Do I reflect upon this fact when I prepare to engage in sin?

❷ Do I attempt to dismiss the sufferings of Jesus when I try to understand what happened during his passion?

❸ How can the brutal sufferings of Christ help me to better understand what is meant by a theology of redemptive suffering?

The
Crowning With Thorns

· · · · · · · · · · · · · · · · · · · ·

"HAIL, KING OF THE JEWS!"

✝ The primary function of the crowning with thorns was not physical pain. Understood by itself, the embedding of the sharp spikes into Jesus' forehead might merely seem another form of bodily harm. However, if we look at the Gospel accounts of Jesus' passion, we see that placing this crown on his head was part of a tactic of humiliation; he was also given a robe and mocked by the soldiers, who scoffed at the notion of his being King of the Jews.

When meditating on the crowning with thorns in the context of the Mass, the first thing we should reflect upon is the inherent sovereignty of the Son of God. Jesus is, as we know, the King of the Jews. This title was one that was used in many ways during the passion of our Lord, and not only by the soldiers who mockingly referred to Jesus using this title. As we learn from John's Gospel, Pilate insisted that the placard placed above the head of our Lord be inscribed with the words: "Jesus of Nazareth, the King of the Jews" (John 19:19–22). Pilate's motivation for doing so is not entirely clear, but we understand from the response of the Jewish officials that this sign was not sufficiently mocking enough for their tastes. They insisted that Pilate change the wording to indicate that such a claim to kingship was just that: a claim and not a reality. Pilate refused. What he had written, he had written.

As we approach the Mass, our response to the sovereignty and kingship of Christ can be looked at in light of the responses of the soldiers, Pilate, and the Jewish officials. Each of these three examples ascribes a type of authority to Jesus that is incomplete or flawed in some way. And yet the way that we acknowledge the authority of Jesus as we approach the Eucharist can often be reflective of the way Jesus himself was approached by these three parties.

In the case of the soldiers, there was an ignorance and misunderstanding as to whom they were dealing with. They didn't recognize Jesus as the Messiah; they merely saw him as another person they were charged to torture and execute. They weren't concerned with the politics or the theology of the situation; they were merely concerned with performing their duty and moving on to the next task. There is a possible connection with their approach to Jesus and the way we sometimes approach the Mass, particularly when we see our obligation to participate in Communion as just that: mere obligation. When we look at Mass in this way, we are dumbing down our participation, mechanically "following orders" like the soldiers, not because we deliberately want to mock Jesus, but because receiving Communion is just "what we do" as Catholics. When we receive the Eucharist in this way, it is because of a failure on our part, as there was in the case of the soldiers, to recognize whom it is that we are dealing with.

Pilate's response to the kingship of Jesus is significantly more complex than that of the soldiers. In his mind, his political fate didn't rest so much in the hands of the leader of some province he'd been assigned to oversee as much as it did with Caesar, his ultimate boss. He acknowledged Christ's conditional sovereignty in a distracted and backhanded sense. Christ was not a supreme authority to Pontius Pilate; but there was a sense in which Pilate wanted to grant him a certain measure of authority, so long as it didn't threaten Pilate's own authority.

It is Pilate's crowning of Jesus that is often reflective of our own, in the sense that we grant Christ a marginal measure of authority as we approach him in the Eucharist. Perhaps we know our weaknesses and failings as we approach the sacrament. Perhaps we shove them to the back of our minds, thinking that we can keep them compartmentalized for the duration of the time we spend at Mass so that we can revisit them once we've dealt with the impending awkward and confrontational communal experience with our eucharistic Lord. Perhaps we really just want to make sure, as Pontius Pilate did, that chaos and conflict are avoided and that we are not convicted beyond our own convenience. If we approach the Mass in this way, it is not the authority of Jesus that we reverence but our own authority over our own situations that we are attempting to preserve.

The last, and perhaps most sinister way of falsely crowning Christ is connected with the synagogue officials. They had a deliberate will to execute Jesus that overrode any inclination for dialogue. They had seen his miracles. They had witnessed the authority he exercised over unclean spirits. They had a hostility toward him, not because he was a threat to the religion of Abraham, Isaac, and Jacob—he had come to fulfill, not abolish the law—but because he was a threat to the status quo.

In case after case, encounters with Christ as he walked this earth resulted in changed life after changed life. Even the Scribes and Pharisees had witnessed these miracles. The hemorrhaging woman, the paralytic lowered through the roof, the blind Bartimaeus, none of these were able to walk away from their contact with Jesus without being radically and substantially changed. The one significant aspect of the response of so many of the Pharisees and Jewish officials which differed from that of so many of the rest of the crowds was that they refused to let their encounter with Christ change the way they looked at reality. Saint John Vianney once used the analogy of the sun to explain this phenomenon, saying that the same heat that softened wax also served to harden clay. The miracles of Jesus revolutionized the worldviews of those with faith, but for those without faith, their hearts only became increasingly hard.

In our own experience, a divine miracle occurs at each Mass; the bread and wine become the body, blood, soul, and divinity of Jesus. Our approach to this encounter with the sovereignty of the Lord can take on either the character of the crowds, of Pilate, or the Pharisees. We can walk away from our eucharistic encounter with Jesus completely and radically changed, or, like the lukewarm Pilate or the hostile Sanhedrin (the Jewish court who insisted upon Christ's crucifixion), we can encounter this miracle and walk away even more hardened and more resistant to change.

Human beings have, in their nature, a tendency to want to grant some kind of sovereignty to someone or something. If Christ is not the supreme authority in our lives, something else will be: media choices, carnal or lustful appetites, or perhaps our work or social schedules. The same axiom can be applied to the way we approach the sacrifice of the Mass; we become soldier-like mockers of the authority of Jesus, dismissive Pilate-like secularists, or obstinately blind to the sovereignty of Christ as were the Sanhedrin. Wherever we are, whoever we are, we are always eager to grant someone or something authority over our thoughts, words, or actions. Such is the human way of looking at reality. We do not sit objectively above our worlds, deciding coldly which things we will devote ourselves to; rather, we yield to the loudest and most persistent demands on our thoughts from without: finances, family, the fate of our favorite sports team. Fortunately, at every Mass, we have a renewed opportunity to give Christ sovereignty over the way we approach him individually when we re-encounter his passion, death, and resurrection in the Eucharist.

REFLECTION QUESTIONS

❶ Does the way I approach Communion resemble the attitudes of either the soldiers, Pilate, or the Sanhedrin?

❷ Are there aspects of my life that I allow to have more authority than Jesus when I approach the Mass?

❸ How can I adjust my understanding of the sovereignty of Christ so as to better honor him when I receive the Eucharist?

The
Carrying of the Cross
· ·
"TAKE MY YOKE UPON YOU."

✝ There is no aspect of Christ's passion that does not hold symbolic spiritual significance, and one of the most powerful examples of this is Christ's carrying the wooden cross to Golgotha as a symbol of the sin and sorrow he also carried there on behalf of us. Isaiah 53 tells us that it was not merely a physical burden that Jesus bore, but the burden of our infirmities that he bore as well. In some translations of Isaiah 53:4, the word is translated "took up," as if to indicate the voluntary initiative of the "suffering servant" in bearing the burden. Jesus encourages us to employ such initiative as a bare minimum for being his disciple: "If any want to become my followers, let them deny themselves and take up their cross and follow me" (Mark 8:34).

Catholic liturgy is processional by design. We walk in a line together at Mass to receive holy Communion. We process solemnly, because we know that what awaits us at the altar is nothing less than the death of Jesus. Frequently we only bear our own burdens as we walk; occasionally we bear a burden or two on behalf of others as we approach the altar. It is impossible then to imagine the weight Jesus carried to his own sacrifice, as he was dragged down by the sin and sorrow of all of humanity simultaneously. No wonder he fell three times in the process.

At a certain point, it became clear that Jesus would not be able to carry his cross alone and survive to suffer the torture of crucifixion, and so Simon, a Cyrenian from North Africa, was pulled from the crowd to assist. Accounts from the Synoptic Gospels of Matthew, Mark, and Luke tell us that Simon did not volunteer for this task. He was, as they put it, ordered to carry the cross. And yet Simon, the first recognized African saint, was transformed by this act. The evidence of this transformation is not immediately noted in any of the Gospels, but tradition holds that Simon was among the "men of Cyrene" mentioned in the Acts of the Apostles who preached the Gospel to the Greeks. For Simon, the order to carry the cross, which initially came from outside, developed into a personal mission to take up his own cross as a voluntary disciple of Jesus.

So often we think that our religion is our business and our decision, and in a sense, it is. We choose our parish, we choose which Mass we want to attend, and we choose how to speak and act in accordance with the tenets of our faith, some of us doing so in the same way that people choose entrees at a breakfast bar. And while we cannot deny the gift of free will given to us by God, we at the same time cannot dismiss the blatant words of Jesus in John 15:16: "You did not choose me but I chose you." Simon was chosen by Christ to carry the cross before he chose to preach the Gospel to the Greeks. In the same way, our very ability to approach Jesus in the Eucharist is a choice we make because we have been chosen. Faith, we understand, is a gift and not a merit.

Jesus carried his cross as an individual, but his suffering was not merely individual. We know that he met his mother and other holy women along the way, whose sorrows have been recorded by the Evangelists. Simon, though compelled to share in this sorrow, contributed his own strength when the weight of the cross became more than our Lord could bear. In the same way, when we are called to take up our individual crosses, we never do so in isolation unless we impose isolation upon ourselves. If all Christians are called to take up their crosses, then all Christians have some sense, however small, of what this calling entails. As such, we can use our mutual experience of sacrifice and suffering as a way of better understanding what it means to be the Body of Christ.

This is the way we should look at the parishioners around us at Mass. Each baptized Catholic who attends Mass alongside us is someone who at some point has seen value in sacrifice, either for themselves or for others. Hence, each person who shows up at Mass is a person who is bearing a voluntary Christian burden: some small, some great. These are the people who, with us, fight the tendency to carry our cross out of obligation, longing rather to do as Jesus did: "…for the sake of the joy before him… [he] endured the cross" (Hebrews 12:2).

Prior to his crucifixion, Jesus was stripped of his garments. In the tenth station of Saint Alphonsus Liguori's *Way of the Cross*, he writes this prayer: "My innocent Jesus, by the torment you suffered in being stripped of your garments, help me to strip myself of all unnecessary attachment to earthly things, that I may give all my love in you who are so worthy of my love."

Detachment and our inability to attain it is prhaps never more evident than at Mass. During this time when we are supposed to be recalling the most important and eternally significant aspects of our lives as Catholics, we are often recalling just about everything else: unfinished responsibilities at work, petty judgments of fellow parishioners, the fates of various characters on reality TV. And as we get in line to process toward the blessed sacrament, as Jesus processed toward Golgotha, we should remember that this is our last chance to clear our heads and to focus on what we are actually doing. If this whole time our minds have wandered in and out of a myriad of thoughts (distaste for liturgical music, hopes related to the afternoon's football game, what to have for lunch), this is the last best opportunity to abandon all of that, if only for a moment, and prepare to enter into the mystry at hand.

It is no mistake that Saint Alphonsus links detachment with the carrying of the cross. Distractions and misplaced affections are only a couple of forms of the burden that Jesus offers to bear for us, just as he bore the wood of the cross. And as we walk the path, however short, carrying our crosses, however heavy, to the altar, then is the time to walk alongside Jesus, as Simon did, carrying the cross so as to hand it back to Jesus, who will perfect and complete the process.

REFLECTION QUESTIONS

❶ How am I being called to suffer in ways that may prove redemptive?

❷ What attachments need to be stripped from me just as the garments of Jesus were stripped?

❸ How can I better understand my procession toward the eucharistic sacrifice as a way of entering into Christ's journey toward his crucifixion?

The Crucifixion

. . . .
"THE SUN'S LIGHT FAILED."

✝ The death of the Lord is central to the Catholic faith. It is the death that we are reminded of repeatedly at each eucharistic sacrifice. It is what Saint Paul was talking about when he described his ministry to the Corinthians: "For I decided to know nothing among you except Jesus Christ, and him crucified" (Corinthians 2:2).

There is no priesthood without sacrifice. The definition of priesthood subsists in the responsibility to preside over a death pleasing to God. This is the case in any religion that contains within it a priesthood, whether Christian or pagan. Even ancient Judaism recognized that there were certain consecrated persons that, when they stood over the slaughter, were able by the power of God to make holy the death that they were witnessing. This is the essential nature of priesthood, and our insistence on consecrating people toward this end is indicative of how important we see this particular vocation.

However, as Catholics, we know that the death of Jesus that we proclaim at Mass is not like the death of any other sacrificial victim in any other religion. In other religions, even in the Jewish one that Jesus himself practiced, a new victim had to be presented at each sacrifice. There was an understanding that sin and impurity had consequences, and those consequences were mortal. Cattle, sheep, doves, pigeons, and other animals died by the thousands in attempts to atone for human failings. But at the sacrifice of the Messiah, those inadequate sacrifices ceased.

A cow is only capable of so much. A cow does not possess reason, nor would a cow willingly bear the spiritual burdens of a broken humanity. A cow is not divine, no matter what eastern proclivities might lay claim to the contrary. A cow is a cow, and as such, is capable of cow-like things. Therefore, the sacrifice of a cow can only accomplish cow-like redemption. But, as Saint Paul says in 1 Corinthians 13:10: "…when the complete comes, the partial will come to an end." In this case, perfection in sacrifice means none other than the sacrifice of God himself, in the person of Christ Jesus.

The sacrificial death of Jesus is so important that it is referenced at numerous points during the Mass. In the Gloria, we refer to Jesus as the Passover "Lamb of God," a direct reference to his sacrificial nature. In the Nicene Creed, we explicitly call to mind that he was crucified under Pontius Pilate, that he suffered, died, and was buried. The first sentence of the Mystery of Faith which we proclaim at the close of the eucharistic consecration is the fact that Christ has died. And as we prepare to receive Jesus himself in holy Communion, we acknowledge him as the Lamb of God who takes away the sins of the world, proclaiming the fulfillment and replacement of the insufficient sacrifices of the millions of lambs slain for Israel that were unable to take away anything more than individual or national sin, and only temporarily at that.

And if the verbal references to the sacrifice of Jesus weren't enough, one only has to look around one's Church to be supplied with a number of visual reminders of the sacrificial death of our

Lord. Crucifixes adorn tabernacles, stained glass windows, side chapels, and even the occasional holy water font. The Church in her very architecture is forcing us to gaze upon this scandal of the cross, which, as Saint Paul says, serves as foolishness for the abstractly logical and a stumbling block for the success-oriented. Some think it ridiculous that a god could die; some think it even more ridiculous to focus on such a death. Some see the death of Jesus as an embarrassing but necessary part of salvation history. But the Church in her wisdom knows that resurrection is the direct byproduct of crucifixion, and that there is absolutely no way around the cross.

The central event of the Old Testament, the event that is mentioned in almost every book of the Bible, is the Exodus of the Hebrews from the land of Egypt, and the central event of the Exodus itself is the Passover. The fact that Jesus used this central event of the Jewish faith as the means by which to institute the most important sacrament of the Catholic faith shows that he had not a distaste for Judaism, but a deep respect for it. As Christ himself stated, he did not come to abolish the law, but to fulfill it. Part of the obligation of Jews was to carry the commemoration of Passover from generation to generation. By Jesus offering himself as the perfect Passover Lamb and instructing his Apostles to maintain perpetual remembrance of him as such, he was bringing Christian fulfillment to the Jewish tradition.

For the Israelites who covered their houses with the blood of lambs at the first Passover, they and their families were spared from death and called out of imprisonment and toward a promise of inheriting the land for which they were destined. When we as Catholics partake of the blood of Jesus, the spotless Paschal Lamb, we are given victory over death and take another step closer to our inheritance in the eternal kingdom of God which he has foreordained for all who respond to his call.

It has been addressed earlier in this book that Catholics are often accused of morbidity. We are the sort of religion that looks at the way Saint Apollonia's persecutors broke her teeth off with pincers before killing her and go on to declare her the patron saint of dental patients. We contemplate the grilling of Saint Lawrence and name him the patron saint of cooks. We speak out against the culture of death, and yet, we come from a tradition known for its lack of fear regarding death. Jesus died naked and lacerated. This must confuse outsiders to the faith when they see us Catholics using what might objectively be called the most embarrassing moment in Christian history as our proudest symbol.

We know that there is a difference between holy and unholy death. Holy death must be seriously contemplated; the holiest of deaths most seriously so. The Mass reminds us weekly, even daily, that there is no death holier than the death of the Lord, and it is that death that we proclaim at every Mass, in every parish, in every part of the world, until he comes in glory.

REFLECTION QUESTIONS

❶ How can I come to terms with any discomfort I might have regarding the violent death of Jesus?

❷ How seriously do I consider the ultimate sacrifice of Jesus when it comes to thinking about the sacrifices I need to make in order to draw more closely to him?

❸ How prominently does the death of Jesus play into my understanding of what it means to embrace the life of Jesus?

The GLORIOUS MYSTERIES

The
Resurrection

. . . .

"THE FIRSTBORN FROM AMONG THE DEAD"

✝ Traditionally, Jesus is depicted in art as having a relatively monochromatic wardrobe. From Fra Angelico's *Maddona and Child* to Lhermitte's *Supper at Emmaeus* to Dali's *The Christ of St. John of the Cross*, we see him most often girded in white cloth. With the exception of crucifixion scenes (which have him dressed in only a loincloth) or perhaps the portions of his passion in which a purple robe is thrust mockingly upon him, the Lord is more often than not artistically depicted as a white-clad Messiah, and never are these robes more radiant than in portraits from Bellini, Rubens, Rembrandt, and many more in their paintings of the resurrected Christ.

We reflect this radiant whiteness of the resurrected Jesus in several ways in our churches during the Easter season, which begins with the steadily increasing glow of candles at the Easter vigil as Holy Saturday draws to a close. Our sanctuaries are decorated with white banners, flowers, and candles. Even the priest himself wears white liturgical vestments for the fifty days of Easter, as a reference to those so often associated with the risen Jesus. The flame of the white paschal and baptismal candles reminds us of the life-giving light of resurrection. The white baptismal robes of infants are a symbol of new life in Christ, a foreshadowing of the eternal life that the faithful will someday share in the resurrection.

Resurrection might seem a confusing thing to celebrate at Mass, particularly because the central event of the eucharistic liturgy is the re-presentation of the death of the Lord. And yet, the mystery of faith that we proclaim at every Mass reminds us that yes, Christ has died, but also, he is risen. And because he is risen, he will come again. Since the Mass is extended through time, we who are stuck in chronology must allow ourselves for a brief moment to see time as God sees it, to be transported to the past sacrifice of Jesus in order to enter into the future victory of Jesus. In doing so, we come to better understand that the resurrection of the Lord is the present reality in which we currently live. And we know that although all of these mysteries are occurring in the eternal present for a God who is not bound by time, it is a future hope that we proclaim when we acknowledge that this risen Christ will come again.

There is no resurrection without death. Saint Paul expresses this in one of his most inspiring and challenging statements from the letter to the Phillippians, where he states the desire to know Christ and "...the power of his resurrection and the sharing of his sufferings by becoming like him in his death, if somehow I may attain the resurrection from the dead" (Philippians 3:10–11).

If our final hope is resurrection, then our immediate hope is a good death. A good death is a death in the context of the sacraments—the kind of death that we so often pray for through the intercession of Saint Joseph, and the kind that inspires such things as the First Friday devotions recommended by our Lord to Saint Margaret Mary of Alacocque for final repentance.

It is one thing to proclaim that it is possible for an all-powerful

God to obtain resurrection from the dead for himself. But at Mass, we make it a point to reflect on the fact that the hope of resurrection is also the sure hope of those who have died in God's favor. These favored ones are the saints, those first in line for a new body, whom we invoke at the eucharistic prayers. This cloud of witnesses encompasses rugged fishermen like Saints Peter and Andrew, as well as meek adolescents like Agnes and Cecilia. Saints from all walks of life, as well as all stages of life, witness the same sacrifice that we ourselves witness at Mass.

These are the holy men and women who accompany us at the eucharistic sacrifice and wait in the same state of joyful hope in which we also wait. In Revelation 6, we see the souls of those who have been slain for their fidelity to the faith expressing their anticipation for the return of Christ, praying for us from beneath the altar. We can make a direct connection between this vision of Saint John the Revelator and the altars of our churches, which so often have placed within them the relics of saints, a practice that dates back to the earliest years of the Church. Hence, at Mass, when we sing the "unending hymn of praise" proclaiming the holiness of God, it is no mere metaphor when we make mention of the saintly praise which joins our own.

We typically gather for Mass in the morning, just as the women who went to honor the crucified Christ also gathered at his tomb in the early hours of the day. For the majority of us who attend Mass, the memory of our awakening from sleep is often still fresh in our minds as we approach the altar to receive holy Communion. We often forget, however, that every awakening from sleep is a foretaste of the resurrection in which the faithful will all take part at the coming of Jesus. Sleep, as it has been referred to, is a small taste of death, a nightly surrender of our consciousness to whatever may befall us as we lie in our beds.

Saint Thérèse of Lisieux was known to drop off into sleep while praying. The over-pious critic might be tempted to criticize the Little Flower for this tendency, but I, for one, see her as a model of holy abandonment in this regard. For those who, like myself, often find the worries and responsibilities of everyday life to be interruptive agents in their sleep patterns, we can admire the saintly trust of Saint Thérèse. She was able to commit this supreme act of surrender, knowing that she could rest peacefully until daybreak, because nothing could happen to her while she slept that could possibly wrench her from the hand of God.

Sleep requires trust, just as death requires trust. Who knows what might happen to us in the night as we doze off, surrendering our consciousness, our vulnerability, and our petty illusions of control? Only a faith in daily resurrection from sleep can allow us to achieve some measure of nightly peace and any semblance of restful sleep. The hope of daily resurrection as a foretaste of the eternal resurrection must be a part of our lives if we are to develop any kind of trust in God as to what we might encounter between death and heaven. As we prepare for this nightly "trust fall," we have to pray about our responsibilities the way Pope John XXIII was remarked to have prayed about his before nodding off: "*Signore, é la vostra chiesa. Vado dormire*" ("It's your Church, Lord! I'm going to bed"). If we can't believe that God will carry us safely into the next morning, how can we trust him to carry us into the eternal daylight of his kingdom at the resurrection?

Before receiving Communion himself, the priest utters the phrase, "The Body (and Blood) of Christ bring me to everlasting life." In speaking these words, the man who stands in the person of Christ is making one of the most profound of all the theological statements in the Mass: that the sacrificed Christ whom he consumes is the pathway to resurrection and that everlasting life is the product of worthy Communion.

What does it mean to practice resurrection? A view of nature can be of assistance here. We know, as Jesus tells us, that "unless a grain of wheat falls into the earth and dies, it remains just a single grain; but if it dies, it bears much fruit" (John 12:24). Temporal death is the necessary prerequisite for eternal life. This is why Catholics for centuries have embraced the crucifix not as a symbol of despair, but as a symbol of hope. As Jesus has instructed us so clearly: "If any want to become my followers, let them deny themselves and take up their cross and follow me. For those who want to save their life will lose it, and those who lose their life for my sake will find it" (Matthew 16:24–25).

REFLECTION QUESTIONS

❶ How can I live with a view of eternity and not just act only in accordance with the circumstances of my present reality?

❷ How can I develop my relationship with the saints who have gone before me so as to better understand the entire Church's share in the resurrection?

❸ What are the situations in my own life that I need to give over to death so as to better enter into a resurrection mentality?

The Ascension

· ·

"A CLOUD TOOK HIM FROM THEIR SIGHT."

✝ Catholicism, as we have noted before, is inherently processional in its liturgical expression. At the beginning of Mass, the priest processes from the back of the Church to the front of the Church. But the priest also makes another journey, one which elevates him from the level of the parishioners, up the steps to the altar. In this, we find the first symbolic representation of the ascension in the Liturgy of the Mass.

The connection with the beginning of Mass and the ascension is perhaps better envisioned in more traditional liturgies, especially where the priest carries incense with him to the altar. The rising of the smoke from the incense is an ancient Jewish symbolism meant to remind us how our prayers rise up to the Father. We even reflect on prayer as an upward motion when we say the *Sursum Corda:* "We lift [our hearts] up to the Lord." For the priest to offer our prayers upward from the altar should call to mind for us how Christ ascended to the right hand of the Father to carry our prayers to him as the true mediator between God and Man. We acknowledge this role of the ascended Jesus in the Gloria: "You are seated at the right hand of the Father; have mercy on us."

The cloud of incense that accompanies the ascendant priest is also reminiscent of the ascension event itself, as Luke tells us in the Acts of the Apostles. The ascending Jesus is hidden by a cloud at his rising.

Jesus tells us in John 12 that when he is lifted up above the earth, he will draw all people unto himself. This "lifting up" of Jesus is hinted at in many ways: his going up the mountain to pray, his proclamation of the kingdom of God from atop a hillside, his transfiguration, even his uplifted body at the crucifixion. Even at Mass, the priest elevates the host at consecration, commemorating the lifting up of Jesus on the cross. Christ's ultimate lifting up, however, is when he ascends to his seat at the right hand of the Father.

We are constantly reminded in our liturgy of a sort of ascendant reality to the kingdom of God. We see the journey from our state to the state for which we were meant as a journey from lowness to highness. This is evoked in the liturgy time and time again, as we glorify God in "the highest." Not only do we mean the "highest" in the sense that our God is the God who supersedes all other gods, but also that the circumstances of the kingdom of God are "above" our own circumstances. In his preaching, Jesus repeatedly refers to the idea that in the kingdom of God, those who are on lower levels will be exalted to higher levels.

To the person who rightly has trouble with geographically locating heaven, it is important to remember that our grasp of the eternal is bound by temporal language. If we want to understand the realm of eternity, the only way to do so is by using temporal language. If we want to understand the spiritual, the only way we can describe it is by using physical language. If we were to take the idea of heaven being "above" literally, we would make the same mistake as those who built the Tower of Babel, who thought that if we could merely climb high enough, we would reach heaven itself, or, conversely, that we could take a shovel and dig to hell.

This is not what we are talking about when we talk about the ascension of Jesus. It is perfectly reasonable to believe the Gospel accounts of Jesus shooting upward after commissioning his disciples. However, at a certain point, we know that the destination of Jesus becomes obscured by a cloud, just as we know that our attempts to explain heaven are limited by our finite language. But we also know this: that we are, as Saint Paul says, called to set our minds on those things which are above, not on earthly things, because that is where Christ is seated at the right hand of the Father (see Colossians 3:1–3).

Saint Paul reminds us that the ascension is connected with the Incarnation. In Ephesians 4:9–10, he writes: "When it says, 'He ascended,' what does it mean but that he had also descended into the lower parts of the earth? He who descended is the same one who ascended far above all the heavens, so that he might fill all things."

As the saying goes, what goes up must come down. In Pauline Christology, it might be appropriate to say that he who has come down must go back up. Jesus mentions this necessity of returning to the Father as the Incarnate second person of the Trinity in order to prepare a place for flesh-and-blood unions such as ourselves in the kingdom of heaven.

A portion of our eucharistic prayers are offered for those who "have gone to their rest in the hope of rising again." And when we use the word "rising," we do so in a dual sense; not only will the friends of God rise from the dead, they will also rise, as did Jesus, to eternal fellowship with the Godhead.

REFLECTION QUESTIONS

❶ How can I see all of Christ's actions as pointing to the hope of ascension to the kingdom of heaven?

❷ How can understanding the way that God views time and place differently than I do help me to better understand the idea that heaven is a mystery?

❸ What insight does the Incarnation of Christ give me about his desire to relate to humanity? How does it help me understand my call to lift my goals and actions toward eternal purposes?

The
Descent of the
Holy Spirit at Pentecost

"HE LIVES WITH YOU AND WILL BE IN YOU."

✝ If the ascension is all about movement from low to high, then Pentecost is all about movement from high to low. As we said before, however, the limits of our language prohibit us from explaining what happened at Pentecost without invoking physical imagery. Perhaps this is why the Holy Spirit is often considered the most difficult person of the Trinity to understand. We know what fathers and sons look like, but the physical approximations of the Holy Spirit in the Bible are more elusive: water, wind, fire, a dove.

One of the ways to better understand the person and work of the Holy Spirit is to look at Pentecost as an image of the Mass: the Holy Spirit descends into a situation where the priesthood of Jesus is present, consecration takes place, and we are sent out of the situation to proclaim the Gospel. This is what happened in the upper room—those first priests of the Church, the Apostles, were unified in prayer, they welcomed the Holy Spirit, and empowered by him, went out to preach the Gospel they had to that point not been adequately empowered to proclaim.

There are many specific moments within the liturgy itself where we make mention of the descent of the Holy Spirit. At the epiclesis, or calling down of the Holy Spirit, the priest asks that the Spirit come upon the gifts that they may become the Body and Blood of Jesus. In this moment, it is the power of the Spirit that transforms the act of the priest. Going back even farther, it was the calling down of the power of the Spirit that made him a priest at his ordination, when he was conferred with the faculties granted to the first Apostles.

The Holy Spirit's role at Mass is largely invisible. It is the Holy Spirit, for example, who was present to inspire the writers of the Scripture whose texts we reflect upon during the Liturgy of the Word. It was the same Holy Spirit that guided the Church to identify which writings were the product of the Spirit's inspiration. Even more, it is the Holy Spirit that has kept the Church from falling since its foundation upon Peter, preserving it infallibly to provide us with the sacraments from the traditional birthday of the Church at Pentecost all the way up to the present day.

It would be fair to say, without disrespect, that the Holy Spirit is the most confusing person of the Trinity. More than one elementary school-age Catholic has heard a catechist refer to the Holy Spirit as "the Paraclete," misheard the title as "parakeet," and wondered why the Spirit was depicted in art as a dove instead. Furthermore, non-Catholic Christians who subscribe to the doctrine of *sola scriptura* or "scripture alone" claim that the most authentic interpretation of Scripture is the one that the Holy Spirit gives to each individual Christian—a belief that has led to the exponential fracturing of Christianity into distinct denominational bodies.

When it comes to the persons of the Trinity, humans, as unions of body and soul, understand Jesus most easily because by his Incarnation, he, like us, is a union of body and soul. God the Father is pure spirit, but the word "father" at least connects with some sort of concrete reality in our mind. The word "spirit," however, can be attached to any number of meanings—many people who have zero connection to the Catholic faith at all claim to be "spiritual" people. "Spirituality" itself is a term that seems to carry a connotation of vagueness and ethereality.

Taking a look at the dispute between the Eastern and Western Churches that led to the schism of 1056 may help us toward a more tangible understanding of the Holy Spirit. This rift between East and West was largely political in nature, but there were theological disagreements thrown into the mix as well. The doctrinal argument at hand had to do with a particular line in the Nicene Creed, which, a thousand years later, Catholics still recite at Mass. In the Eastern parties, it was argued that the Holy Spirit proceeded from the Father, but not the Son. The Western Church (which today is the Roman Catholic Church) maintained that the Holy Spirit proceeds from both the Father *and* the Son. In layman's terms, the love between the Father and the Son is so infinite that it becomes its own person, namely the Holy Spirit. Analogously, we know that the human love between a husband and wife is most perfectly realized in the procreation of another human person, in the form of a child.

If we can understand that the Holy Spirit is the "love child" of the Father and the Son and, at the same time, co-eternal with the Father and the Son, we can better get at a tangible understanding of who the person of the Holy Spirit is. Love, by its nature, entails sacrifice, action, and the will of the greatest good for others. If we understand the Holy Spirit as the perfected love between the Father and the Son who compelled the Apostles at Pentecost, we can get a better grasp on what the role of the Holy Spirit is in the Masses that we experience in our own day and age.

The word "Mass" is derived from the Latin *missa,* meaning "sent." We think of Mass as a gathering, but the Church has always thought of it as a "sending." In my evangelical days, I always referred to congregational gatherings as "church services." That Catholics referred to their gatherings as "Mass" confused me. I thought Masses were so called because this was a setting wherein Catholics "amassed" themselves. Fortunately, the Latin root of the word "Mass" gives striking clarity to what is really meant by the gathering. The root word, *missa*, is also found in the words "missionary," "transmission," and even "missile"—all of which are things that are sent.

This is what the Apostles were dealing with at Pentecost. They experienced a radical encounter with the Holy Spirit, and their response was to share that encounter with the world. In their case, this was literal—because of the gathering of diaspora Jews in Jerusalem for the feast of Pentecost, the people who heard this first preaching of the Apostles were from all over the Roman world: Egypt, Libya, Greece, and beyond. In our case, our radical encounter with the Holy Spirit perhaps calls us to share the Gospel with a more local audience—family, friends, coworkers, the occasional stranger. But in both our cases and that of the Apostles, the mandate is the same: we cannot come into intimate contact with the Spirit of God and remain unchanged.

When Jesus tells the Apostles what to expect of the Holy

Spirit, he describes the Spirit as teacher, guide, and counselor. We might say the same of our pastors, the heirs of the Apostles, as they teach, guide, and counsel the Church through their own anointing in the Holy Spirit at ordination. Some cynics might contend that priests deal with spiritual matters and aren't equipped to tell us how we who occupy the "real world" are supposed to live. But if we understand that they are invested with the same Spirit that empowered the Apostles at Pentecost, we might better respect their office and understand their challenge to us as an echo of Peter's at Pentecost: "Repent, and be baptized every one of you in the name of Jesus Christ so that your sins may be forgiven; and you will receive the gift of the Holy Spirit" (Acts 2:38).

REFLECTION QUESTIONS

❶ How can I move beyond an abstract understanding of the Holy Spirit to a more tangible understanding of him and his work?

❷ What are the ways in which I can view my attendance at Mass as a type of gathering similar to that of the Apostles in the Upper Room as they prepared to receive the Holy Spirit?

❸ How is the Holy Spirit calling and empowering me to proclaim the Gospel with which I have been entrusted?

The
Assumption of Mary

· ·
"HE HAS LIFTED UP THE LOWLY."

✝ The Assumption is one of two mysteries of the rosary not explicitly recorded in the Bible. For this reason, Catholics can sometimes be a little embarrassed by this doctrine. Prior to becoming Catholic, I remember traveling with an art class from my evangelical college to Covington, Kentucky, to see the largest hand-blown stained glass window in the world at the Cathedral Basilica of the Assumption. At the time, having little knowledge of the intricacies of Catholic dogma, I remember snidely commenting, "This is an awfully big church for someone to have built based on an assumption!" Now, as a Catholic, I can more clearly see the implications of the Assumption of Mary on Christian theology, and as a result, am more sensitive to the ways in which these implications are deeply embedded in the Mass.

The Church allows freedom on the question of whether or not Mary ever tasted death. However, all Catholics in line with the Church agree that she has been assumed, body and soul, into heaven. That is why we are able to ask her in the *Confiteor,* wherein we confess our sins communally at the beginning of Mass, that she plead on our behalf for the mercy of God. That is also why we ask her to join her pleas to ours during the eucharistic prayers of the liturgy, an explicit acknowledgement that she is in a unique position to ask her son to show us his favor.

The Mass has been referred to by many as "heaven on earth." The architecture of our churches is meant to reflect heaven. This is sometimes more evident in Baroque, Romanesque, and Neoclassical churches, whose vaulted ceilings and ornate fixtures are intended to reflect the heavenly temple of God. In order to reflect heaven more perfectly, all Catholic churches have statues or portraits of Mary, who was assumed body and soul into heaven and dwells with Jesus in the heavenly temple.

The Gospel accounts tell us that Mary is present at a number of the events we remember as we pray the rosary. We recall that it is Mary who gives birth to Jesus by the power of the Holy Spirit. It is she who received the announcement of his conception and she who visited Elizabeth in the hill country. She presented Jesus at the Temple at her purification, and she and Joseph fretted together for three days when they lost him during a pilgrimage to the same Temple twelve years later. After journeying with him to Calvary, she mourned before the cross as her son breathed his last. And she prayed in expectation in the Upper Room when the Holy Spirit came in power upon the Apostles. If our Catholic faith is not merely about memorizing a set of facts but about encountering a person, then there is no better model of what it means to personally encounter the Godhead than Mary, his mother.

Mary gives us hope. Not only does she give us hope because of *what* she *does* for us, but because of *whom* she *is* for us. She bore the child Jesus, who would suffer, die, resurrect, and ascend. She had a special place of honor in his Incarnation, and as a result, has a special place of honor at his resurrection.

I remember a treasured conversation I had on a hike with my

father shortly after I had decided to become Catholic, wherein I told him of a pending decision to pursue higher education at a university founded by a religious order devoted to Marian theology. My father, a man who shares with me a deep love of Scripture, remarked innocently and without malice that he was unaware that Mary had done any extensive theological writing. My response to him was neither flippant nor mechanical; I shared that Marian theology was not about Mary's thought but rather about her being. I know my father well enough to know that the silence we shared together for the rest of the walk was one steeped in contemplation rather than conflict.

If Mary is the model for us in her obedience, then she must necessarily be the model for us in her reward. If someone was worthy to receive Christ into her womb, it is no leap to accept the strong and early tradition that she was also worthy to share the same bodily assumption as Enoch and Elijah. She, like they, walked and "was no more." Scripture and tradition tell us that there are certain rewards prepared for those who display unprecedented levels of holiness. That the Assumption has gone unrecorded in Scripture is regrettable, just as the definition of trinitarian doctrine is not explicitly recorded in Scripture. However, if the pun can be pardoned, given certain Scriptural precedents, some doctrines can be safely "assumed."

Mary is proof that, by grace, heaven is attainable, even for those of us who don't possess a divine nature. She was granted unique graces in order to bear the son of God, but even the most devoted Mariologists have been careful to point out that she is not divine as is her Son. However, if the ascended Jesus is, as Saint Paul tells us, the first fruit of the realized promise of God, then Mary is the second. She shares our full humanity, and her obedience perfects that humanity. Because of that docility, she is able to have a relationship with Jesus that is more intimate than any of us. Yet her example shows us that the more closely we conform our will to God's, the greater our intimacy with him will be.

REFLECTION QUESTIONS

❶ How does Mary's Assumption serve as a hope for my own admission into the kingdom of heaven?

❷ How can I look to Mary as an ally and intercessor so as to more faithfully complete my own spiritual journey?

❷ How can my Marian understanding move beyond what Mary said and did to who Mary is?

The
Coronation of Mary

✝ "By the mystery of this water and wine," the priest prays as he prepares for consecration, "may we come to share in the divinity of Christ, who humbled himself to share in our humanity." The goal of the Christian life is nothing less than divinization, to become like Christ. This doesn't mean that we become a substitute for him, gaining our own kingdoms (as in Mormon theology), or that we find the secret path to true enlightenment that makes us our own Gods (as in some Gnostic theologies), but rather that we come to share in the kingdom of God as heirs and not as mere tourists or employees.

Mary has pre-eminence among humans in this regard. She is the one who humbled herself to bear the Son of God and was exalted by him at the crucifixion to be the mother of the Church when the dying Jesus told John the Evangelist to behold her as such. She is the one who paves the way for all Christians to take part in the kingdom of God.

The traditional Jewish role of the "queen mother" is a difficult one for us to understand in a democratic society. There is something especially American about a reluctance to submit to non-democratic authority. We like the possibility, however illusory, of being able to fire our rulers. The pick-and-choose method of many Catholics when it comes to following Church teaching indicates that we often prefer to serve Jesus, not as the

King of Kings in the kingdom of God, but as the president of presidents in the democratic republic of God. Radical submission is not exactly a non-negotiable element of our national makeup.

However, something else that we have trouble understanding is that in monarchic cultures, profound honor does not necessarily mean absolute power. In Jewish tradition, the "Queen Mother," who had given birth to the ruling monarch, was a highly respected figure. No one would doubt that whoever was king of Israel or Judah at a given time had the final word on all temporal matters under his jurisdiction. But show me a Judaic king who didn't give serious consideration to the requests of his own mother, and I'll show you a king whose reign was either destructive, insignificant, or cut short by an untimely death.

Such is the role of Mary in the kingdom of heaven. Jesus, as the liturgy states, humbled himself to share in our humanity so that we might share in his divinity. It could be said that Mary humbled herself *despite* her humanity, and as a result, has become the first to taste the promise of divinity. She is not a part of the Godhead; we know that nothing can be added to or subtracted from the Trinity. But if, as Saint Paul tells us, the prayers of the righteous man have great effect, then the prayers of the divinely appointed woman, Mary, have a superlative degree of effect in the kingdom of God.

In any society, when a man becomes king, his entire family becomes royalty of some kind, deserving of honor. It is for this reason that we honor Mary in "May Crownings," not because she is divine, but because she has blood ties to the Son of God, and as such is deserving of honor. We are children of God who respond to his call and are baptized, but it is by a spiritual grace that we are adopted into the family of God. Mary's connection to the family of God is both spiritual *and* physical. This gives us reason to honor her, not as we honor God himself, but as we would honor the most exemplary person among us, because that is who Mary is. Is it not a shame, then, that we so often give more honor to our temporal political leaders than we do to the Mother of God?

Logically speaking, if Jesus sits at the right hand of the Father, then we can reasonably deduce that Mary sits at the right hand of Jesus. Our Lord told James and John that it was not for him to determine who sat at his right and left, but that it was left to the will of his Father. And given the fact that it was God the Father who selected Mary to bear the newborn King, we can fairly say that this designation makes her royalty, though not divinity, in the kingdom of heaven.

Many queens are not royalty by birth. But if they marry into a royal family, they become grafted into the royal life. Her Serene Highness, the late Princess Grace of Monaco, was a film star who, when she caught the eye of Prince Rainier, was immediately drawn into participation in the royal bloodline. Prior to that moment, she had not been royalty; but as soon as she was selected to bear the children of Prince Rainier, she became royalty. In the case of Mary, she was selected at the moment of her conception to bear the Son of God himself. It defies logic to think of God the Father sitting in heaven, sifting through resumes of potential bearers of his Son, and weeding out candidates whenever they did something dumb. God did not merely select Mary out of a lineup of prospects and recruits; he *ordained* her. And any proper understanding of vocation must take into account that a calling is based on whom we have from all history been created to be. If, from all history, Mary was created to be the mother of the King of Kings, then we must assume that royalty was attached to her from all eternity.

Finally, Mary reminds us that there is such a thing as sovereignty outside of ourselves. It is easy to believe that an omnipotent, omniscient, omnipresent God is greater than we; it is harder to make ourselves humble enough to believe that other human beings are greater, even though the facts of Mary's role in the plan of our salvation speak for themselves when it comes to her superiority among Christians. The role of Mary in salvation history should inspire humility in us; it was she who was chosen from all of humanity to be the channel through which God's Son would enter the world. We didn't make the cut. And yet, she also reminds us that the crown of victory is something that is attainable, even for humans, so long as we follow her example and make ourselves docile to the will of God, responding as she did: "Be it done unto me according to your word."

REFLECTION QUESTIONS

❶ How do Christian aspirations of divinity differ from divine aspirations of other religions?

❷ How do my views of democratic honor and authority taint my view of honor and authority in the kingdom of God?

❸ What does the coronation of Mary as Queen of Heaven tell me about my own role in the kingdom of heaven?

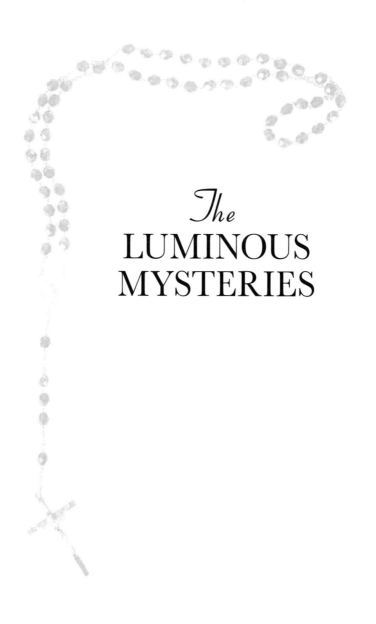

The
LUMINOUS
MYSTERIES

The
Baptism of the Lord

· ·
"THIS IS MY SON, THE BELOVED."

† The theme of baptism saturates the Mass, all pun intended. The moment we set foot in our churches, we bless ourselves with holy water as a reminder of our baptism; we perform the same act as we leave. For good measure during the Easter season, the priest sprinkles us with holy water in order to make sure we're good and reminded that there was a point at which we were officially and sacramentally welcomed into the Body of Christ.

Water itself is a sign of life. When scientists search for life on other planets, the first indication of hope is the presence of water in any state of matter. The life of the Trinity enlivens us at our own water baptism. It is Jesus who tells us in Matthew 28 that in order to become his disciples, we must be baptized in the trinitarian form. As Philip catechizes the Ethiopian in Acts 8, the fact that a source of water is nearby causes the Ethiopian to practically leap out of his chariot, compelled by his thirst for the life-giving graces of baptism.

We also know, as we approach Communion, that it is our baptism that enables us to do so. Baptized Catholics are subjected to ongoing catechesis to prepare them to bear the full weight of what occurs when they receive the Eucharist. Even those who have been validly baptized in other Christian communions are forbidden to receive the Catholic Eucharist, because the validity of their baptism has not been verified by the sacrament of confirmation. We want them to know what they're getting into.

Jesus, however, was born neither with original sin nor the concupiscience that accompanies it. Why, then, was he baptized? There are many possible explanations. However, at least one reason for Jesus to ask for John's baptism is consistent with his desire for Incarnation; he wants to identify with us. Baptism makes us part of the Christian community; Christ, though sinless, joins us in this, just as Christ submits himself to death. He does this not because *he* needs it, but because *we* need it. This is just one of the many tangible examples of the total and perpetual self-gift that sustains the Trinity.

The gift of baptism is foreshadowed throughout the Scriptures: the Spirit of God hovering over the waters of creation, the dove that returned to the ship-bound Noah bearing an olive branch, the salvation of the Israelites who passed safely through the Red Sea, the washing of Naaman the Syrian in the Jordan to cure his leprosy. There are aspects of each of these Old Testament accounts that pave the way for a baptismal understanding of how God has ordained that we die and rise with him as new creations, cleansed from a spiritual font.

John distinguished his baptism from that of Jesus: "'I baptize you with water for repentance, but….He will baptize you with the Holy Spirit and fire" (Matthew 3:11). John's baptism was one of a ritual gesture of repentance, a visible public symbol that someone was sorry for his or her sins. But the baptism of Jesus, at which the Holy Spirit was present, had a power that went beyond that of a mere social gesture.

Today, the issue of what is meant by baptism is a source of division within many Christian communities. Perhaps the view of the Catholic Church is the most consistent, the most scriptural, and maybe even the most easily understood—any baptism in the name of the Father, Son, and Holy Spirit, when entered into with the correct intention, is valid. As I was preparing to come into the Catholic Church, I was asked to present evidence that I had been baptized in such a manner. When I responded to the priest who received me into the Church that I had been baptized in this way three separate times over the course of my life, I was greeted with incredulity. Catholics don't re-baptize the way that some non-Catholic Christians do. When we remind ourselves of our baptism at each sign of the cross, it is just that—a reminder.

For Christian communities outside of Catholicism who believe in multiple baptisms, it might be fair to say that re-baptism serves the function of a podium confession—it's not treated like a grace-giving event in and of itself, but rather as a public profession of a repentance event that has happened prior to baptism. Hence, for many Christian denominations, baptism is an act not so much of repentance, but of witness.

For Catholics, baptism is meant to be an act of both repentance *and* witness. Not only does baptism cleanse infants of original sin and adult consenters of all sin to that point, but it also shows to all witnesses the power of God's grace in the sacrament.

Some protestant groups, heirs of the Anabaptists who populated Europe during the continental Reformation, have difficulty believing that baptism can have any gracious effect on an infant. I have had this conversation a few times with a non-Catholic but theologically generous brother of mine, who has acknowledged that neither an infant, child, or perhaps even some teenagers or adults can have full knowledge of what's going on when they are presented for baptism. But sometimes there are certain spiritual medications that have effect upon us even if we don't fully comprehend them. As the analogy goes, not everyone can save themselves from a burning building—every now and then, we have to trust a rescuer (in the case of infants, a parent) to do for us what we would do for ourselves if we had the good sense to do so.

Baptism is our ticket to the eucharistic feast. There is no worthy Communion without valid baptism. Some of us were baptized shortly after our birth. For those in this category, there is usually either a sense of gratitude, resentment, or apathy—gratitude because someone saw fit to rescue us from original sin as a firefighter rescues a child from a burning house, resentment because we had no say in the matter ourselves, or apathy because we don't believe that baptism matters in the first place. But the first rule of being a good houseguest is honoring the request of the host, and the host which we receive has indicated through his Church that baptism is the ticket we must show at the door before entering the banquet. We experience the same necessary exclusivity in a number of ways in the everyday: we may purchase tickets to a game of our own volition, we may have been given them by surprise, or we may have bought them and neglected to use them. In the case of baptism, it is the same; no matter how we acquired our tickets, we must present them upon entry if we expect to legitimately participate in the proceedings.

Baptism establishes our Catholic identity. At baptism, we are called by name. Our membership in the Body of Christ is confirmed. We are now, as Saint Paul tells us, functioning organs in the Body of Christ. And, as in any organization, membership in that body bears with it responsibility. For we who have been baptized, that responsibility is nothing less than to daily live as Christ for the sake of his body, honoring our baptismal call to die to sin so as to be raised in Christ.

REFLECTION QUESTIONS

❶ When was I baptized? Was I aware of what I was getting myself into at the time?

❷ What is my attitude toward the circumstances under which I was baptized?

❸ How do I view my membership in the Body of Christ as opposed to the ways in which I view my membership in other organizations?

The
Wedding at Cana

· ·

"DO WHATEVER HE TELLS YOU."

✝ The first miracle of Christ takes place in the context of community. The wedding guests at Cana gathered because of a common connection to the couple who were being married. Miracles, as Jesus shows in this first adult display of his power, are not merely for the individual.

When we gather at Mass, we gather based on our common connection to Christ. Our individuality is evident, and our connection with Christ in the Eucharist takes place on the most personal and individual levels. But it also takes place in the context of the greater reality of the Body of Christ, meaning that we commune not just with those gathered in the chapels and sanctuaries alongside us, but also with Catholics around the world and Catholics who have been part of the Church throughout Christian history.

In John's Gospel, just before Jesus' first miracle at Cana, we see him gathering his first disciples to him: Andrew, Peter, Philip, Nathanael. As the beginning of the Cana narrative tells us, these newly recruited disciples are on hand for the wedding feast. By their attendance, these first priests of the Church are being prepared for the mystery of wine and blood by the mystery of water and wine. They are part of the community on hand to witness a miraculous foreshadowing of the Eucharist; as we recall in our eucharistic prayers, they are likewise present at each eucharistic miracle that we witness in our own day and age.

Weddings tend to assemble an almost awkwardly diverse cast of characters from two often extremely different families. Perhaps that's why alcohol is so abundant at most weddings—for many invitees, it's hard to find a common connection with the other half of a room without at least a little loosening. It would not be outside of the realm of orthodoxy to suggest that this might have been on Jesus' mind as he added his own enlivenment to the feast.

At my own wedding, such enlivenment was certainly necessary. As someone in the process of converting to Catholicism, and as the only person on my invited side of the family who had endeavored to do so, I was certainly self-conscious about how all the non-Catholics on the "Joseph side" of the seating arrangements would handle the ceremonial proceedings. To top it off, most of my family members in attendance at my wedding were from the Bible Belt and were attending a Catholic Mass for the first time in their lives. This would have been awkward enough as it was, but, as readers are likely aware, Catholic liturgies are by their very nature "call-and-response" occasions and require crowd participation, even if large portions of the crowd might not know how they should participate.

One of those "call-and-response" moments, the recitation of the Our Father during our wedding service, served to amplify the awkwardness of the situation. At Mass, Catholics are used to pausing during the Lord's Prayer at the end of the phrase, "deliver us from evil." We know that this is the point where the officiator says a few words invoking the mercy of God and ushers us into the doxology. However, the vast majority of non-Catholic Christians are unused to pausing at this point. So it was that the "Joseph side" of the sanctuary began to ascribe the "Kingdom, Power, and Glory" to Jesus while the "Mary side," as well as the officiating deacon, looked on in silent discomfort and wondered nervously as to what the next liturgical step should be.

Perhaps the couple being married at Cana (whose names are not revealed to us in the Scriptures) had similar episodes of liturgical awkwardness in their own wedding. We don't have any evidence of this, but the personal experience of most wedding attendees bears witness to the account that in many a case, there is a weird tension that hangs over the union of two families every time the sacrament of matrimony is celebrated. Two entire families full of two new entire groups of unique personalities are being combined, and the two parties involved are faced with a seemingly endless set of unknowns regarding the addition of a new extended family into their own. Hence, it is not beyond the realm of orthodoxy to suggest that Jesus, knowing humans better than they know themselves, turned water into wine at least partially because he knew that livening up the party would help break the tension of what might otherwise be an uncomfortable sacramental combination of families. I tend to believe that in this act, our Lord recognized not only the value of weddings, but also of wedding receptions.

As at Cana, Jesus requests that we present gifts to him at Mass, not because he needs them, but because we need to offer them. In Saint Luke's account of the wedding, Jesus requests jars filled with water that will be transformed into the best wine of the feast. At Mass, we offer wine, which we acknowledge as the offered work of human hands and which will become the Blood of Christ. But it is first the fruit of the vine, a gift to us. Through human processes, we are empowered by God to transform grown grapes into wine and give the gift we have been given back to the giver, who transforms it further into the best vintage of the celebration.

It is significant to note that the water pots requested by Jesus were ritual vessels, used for purification. John's decision to include this detail is perhaps an acknowledgement of the eucharistic significance of this miracle. As paragraph 1416 of the *Catechism of the Catholic Church* tells us, the reception of Holy Communion in a state of grace forgives venial sin. Jesus' miracle of transforming water from purified vessels into wine foreshadows the sacramental cup that serves as an agent of our own purification of venial sin.

As we have noted, the rosary connects us directly with Mary, who intercedes alongside us before her Son. The exchange between Jesus and Mary in John 2 is significant—it shows that Jesus hears and honors the requests of his mother. It is important to understand the dynamic between Jesus and Mary in this passage in a way that neither trivializes nor objectifies their relationship. We shouldn't make the mistake of thinking that Jesus had planned to change the water into wine all along, independent of his mother's ideas, and that his response to Mary's request exhibited a sort of impatient embarrassment on Jesus' part; we might end up mistakenly thinking that he didn't have control of the situation or perhaps had no control over his mother. On the other hand, we shouldn't deduce from this vignette that Mary is like a doorbell that we can ring and be granted automatic favors from Jesus. Rather, this interaction at Cana is one of the most poignant of all Gospel accounts when it comes to showing the relationship between the Son of God and the Mother of God.

It is reasonable, even logical, to interpret Mary's address to Jesus not as a complaint, but as an acknowledgement of her Son's power. One can almost picture an exchange of knowing looks between Jesus and Mary. When Jesus tells Mary that his hour has yet to come, her reaction is not one of frustration. She has known Jesus for thirty years at this point and knows how to read between the lines of Jesus' statements. That's why her response is not one of argument but rather of trust, hence her instruction to the servants: "Do whatever he tells you."

Mary's instruction to the servants at the wedding feast in Cana also applies to us as we attend the eucharistic feast. Over the gifts of the altar, we invoke the entire communion of saints, but we say Mary's name first—as though to remind us of her directions to the servants the first time Jesus performed a miracle involving wine.

REFLECTION QUESTIONS

❶ How can I view the Mass as both an individual and communal event?

❷ What gifts of mine can I present to Jesus, praying that he transform them in order to make them more fruitful?

❸ Through the lens of their recorded exchange at the wedding at Cana, how can I model my relationship with Jesus after Mary's relationship with him?

The
Proclamation of the
Kingdom of God

. . . .

"IT IS RIGHTEOUSNESS."

✝ When the disciples of Jesus asked how they should pray, Jesus gave them the Our Father, one of the principal petitions of which involves asking for God's kingdom to come. But what, exactly, does it mean to ask for this, and what exactly is the kingdom of God?

A skeptic might accuse Jesus himself of being evasive on the question. Our Lord speaks about the kingdom cryptically, never explicitly stating what it is but only what it is like: a mustard seed, a pearl of great price, a sower, yeast. And yet to the earliest Christians, it was clear that at least in one sense, this kingdom was the Church. Saint John proclaims in Revelation 1:6 that he and the Christian communities to whom he writes have been made "a kingdom." John also points out that this kingdom, partially realized even in his day, is one that will not end, a belief we profess every time we recite the Nicene Creed.

In the Beatitudes recorded by Matthew the Evangelist, we see what sorts of people are involved in the kingdom of God: the poor in spirit, those persecuted for righteousness' sake, and those who keep the commandments of Jesus. We acknowledge these kingdom inhabitants in some of our eucharistic prayers, the earliest of which contain litanies of martyrs for the sake of the

Church because of their fidelity to the commandments of Jesus.

Jesus further reminds us of the importance of obedience for those who would be a part of the kingdom: "Not everyone who says to me, 'Lord, Lord,' will enter the kingdom of heaven, but only one who does the will of my Father in heaven" (Matthew 7:21). This is a convicting statement for those of us who plug away mindlessly through the memorized prayers we recite at Mass with our minds occupied by anything *but* the Mass. When we draw our attention away from the altar, the words we say become a mere string of syllables unconnected to our thought processes. And how can we obey if we're not even paying attention to the one who calls us to obey?

There is another kingdom that Jesus addresses during his sermon at the beginning of Matthew's Gospel; that of Satan, whom Jesus is accused of working for. Our Lord corrects the misunderstanding among some as to the identity of his employer, and at the same time, gives us a principle that applies even to the Church: "Every kingdom divided against itself is laid waste."

Jesus reinforces this notion in his high priestly prayer in the garden of Gethsemane that we, the Church, be one. Even a glancing study of Western history since the Reformation shows us that division breeds division. These sixteenth century splits within the Church did not fix the problem; rather, they led to the exponential fracture of Christian unity. We see this continual fracture even in the present, as new, independent Christian communities magisterially unconnected to other Christian communities pop up on almost a daily basis with their own customized doctrines, liturgies, and magisteria. And the often heavy overlap in theology between individual communities doesn't make it any less difficult for non-Catholic Christians to agree on what constitutes a consistent rubric for scriptural interpretation.

One of the reasons religious leaders of Jesus' day did not recognize Jesus as the Messiah was because they did not understand that his kingdom was primarily a heavenly one. In our day and age as Christians, we might be tempted to mock their incredulity and inability to accept the miracles and proclamations of someone who to us seems to be such an obvious fulfillment of the Messianic promise. If so many were healed in front of their eyes, how could they have possibly thought that they had anyone but the Son of God in their midst?

And yet even today, we can sometimes fall into the trap of thinking that Christ's kingdom is an earthly one. We might demand, as did some of his followers, that he immediately take on the prince of this world in final battle, solving once and for all the ills that have plagued our society since the fall. Why should Jesus not correct everything now, if dominion over heaven and earth belongs to him? What is the point in restraint?

This question has made more people into atheists than any other criticism of Christianity. As the argument *contra fide* goes, if God is all powerful and all good, then he can and should orient all situations toward the ultimate good and do so immediately. For nonbelievers, the fact that he hasn't done so either proves impotence or a lack of wisdom on the part of the Almighty, either of which seem a plausible reason for not wanting to trust anything else about him, including accounts of his existence.

Even for faithful Christians, this is one of the hardest entrees of our theological buffet to digest. If the faith of a bleeding Samaritan woman was enough to heal her in the New Testament, then why not the faith of the Catholic parents of a leukemia-stricken child in our own day and age? How can blindness in the Bible be seen as anything other than a visitation of the sins of parents upon a child, or a miscarriage in our day and age be seen as anything other than the curse of a cruel God?

An agnostic friend of mine once argued that people become Catholic because Catholicism provides them with comfort. When she said this, I nearly choked on my food. What casual comfort is there in resigning oneself to emotional pain, physical agony, even death itself?

And yet these are the immediate means that Jesus calls us to embrace before we can experience resurrection. This, to the dismay of the pragmatist, is what the kingdom theology looks like. As human beings, especially postmodern ones, we want, as Wendell Berry says, "the quick profit, the annual raise, vacation with pay...more of everything ready-made." In Western culture, our tendency is to prioritize personal preference over sacrifice to an alarming degree. We demand, as did many in Jesus' day, validation over conviction. Hence, as in the day of Jesus, we who walk the earth now recoil at his challenge: "An evil and adulterous generation asks for a sign..." (Matthew 16:4). Are we evil and adulterous because we ask for help? This question haunts the mind of the majority of those who plan on eventually leaving the faith.

However, if we want to understand the kingdom theology, we have to understand that Jesus offers dramatic miracles to some now and to all later. And in the meantime, he offers himself to us constantly in the subtle miracle of the Eucharist, which is meant to sustain us, especially when we can't hear trumpets or heavenly voices telling us we're following the right path. We must also remember that not everyone who saw the miracles of Jesus became his disciples. Some saw them and were compelled to follow him selflessly, while others tagged along selflessly looking for a handout from a walking miracle vending machine. And in the case of his adversaries, even miracles weren't enough to convince them that he was the Son of God. As a matter of fact, as was the case with Pharaoh during the ten plagues, miracles served to harden rather than soften their hearts. For us to demand that the kingdom of God be realized in our day and age is not an indictment of God in terms of his laxity, but an indictment of us in terms of our impatience.

Thankfully, for us as Catholics, the Mass is not only a chance to individually receive the sacrament of the Eucharist; it is also a place to express our gratitude that this sacrament is not only one of unity with Christ, but also of unity with his Church under the successor of Saint Peter, the one to whom Jesus gave the keys of the kingdom.

In Matthew's Gospel, Jesus proclaims the kingdom of God most elaborately in the Sermon on the Mount. He stands in an elevated position, just as Moses brought the law down to the children of Israel from Mount Sinai. We too recognize the authority of the priest to proclaim to us the teachings of God from an elevated position as the *alter Christus,* the one who acts in the person of Christ *for* us in order to bring the person of Christ *to* us. And we, like those who sat at the feet of Jesus as he proclaimed the kingdom of God in first-century Palestine, must sit at the feet of these men selected by Jesus as they remind us of our responsibility to bring about the kingdom today.

REFLECTION QUESTIONS

❶ In what ways can I better understand the kingdom of God so as to better bring about the kingdom of God?

❷ How can I better understand my role in the kingdom of God as a subject of a king, rather than as a voter in a democracy?

❸ How can I do my part to encourage unity rather than division in the Church as I work toward the proclamation of the kingdom?

The
Transfiguration

· ·

"IT IS GOOD THAT WE ARE HERE."

✝ Aside from perhaps the annunciation, there may be more theological meat packed into the transfiguration of our Lord than in any of the other mysteries we meditate upon during the rosary. The transfiguration prefigures the ascension in its foreshadowing of the eternal mission of Jesus, and likewise hints at the realized kingdom of God where Jesus reigns in ultimate glory. It is maybe one of the strangest mysteries to meditate upon but also one of the most important.

When Jesus was transfigured on the mountain, he was flanked by Moses and Elijah, two of the most prominent figures in the Old Testament. Moses was the man God chose to deliver his law to the people of Israel, and Elijah was considered the greatest of the Hebrew prophets. To see Jesus transfigured between them was visual expression to Peter, James, and John of what Jesus meant when he told them that he was the fulfillment of the Law and the Prophets.

The transfiguration is also a reminder that we cannot understand Jesus outside of the context of the Old Testament. Jesus was not sent to sweep away all the theological confusion that had ever occurred in human history, and for the first time since creation, tell us the truth about God. Rather, he came to bring all the information God had given humanity about himself up to that point into better understanding. Readers of mystery novels often enjoy trying to piece together the clues left for them by an author in order to try guess at how a mystery might culminate. A truly gifted mystery writer can come up with an ending so brilliant that a reader will walk away astounded. The Gospels tell us of the astonishment of Peter, James, and John on Mount Tabor as they saw the mystery of Jesus' glory revealed before them.

On the altar of eucharistic sacrifice, we see the mystery of Christ's passion, death, and resurrection revealed before us. Our readings from the Liturgy of the Word are arranged to show us that the Old and New Testaments are in harmony with one another and not opposed to one another, and that taken together, they become a key to better understanding this mystery. If we pay attention to these Scriptures as they are proclaimed to us at Mass, we can see the genius of the proclaimed Word of God as we prepare to receive the Incarnate Word of God. Like Peter, we should desire to enter more deeply into this mystery, and affirm, with him, that "it is good that we are here."

Luke's Gospel tells us that as Jesus was being transfigured, "Now Peter and his companions were weighed down with sleep; but since they had stayed awake, they saw his glory and the two men who stood with him" (Luke 9:32). Mass, especially Sunday Mass, often occurs on an early morning for us after what may have been a late Saturday night at the end of an exhausting week. The pace of our routines is often rushed, while the Mass is a slow, meditative prayer. For those of us who are so used to a rapid-fire work and social environment, we may at times find ourselves nodding off during the liturgy. But the experience of Peter, James, and John reminds us that if we stay awake, we will be able to witness a mystery that we might otherwise miss, namely Jesus revealed to us in the sacrament of the altar.

At the end of Saint John's Gospel, he notes that if everything about Jesus' life were to be recorded, no library could hold the necessary volumes. On one level, I can appreciate this. However, out of all the aspects of Jesus' life that are omitted from the Gospels, I most wish that one of the disciples had written down the verbal exchange between Jesus, Moses, and Elijah. Was their conversation marked by shock or familiarity? Were they discussing how Jesus was about to face death? If I were Moses and had been summoned to Mount Tabor in that moment, what would have been my first question? Unfortunately, the wisdom of the Holy Spirit has seen fit to exclude the specific details of this exchange from the canon of Scripture, so we must conclude that these conversations, like the transfiguration itself, are a mystery.

The transfiguration is nothing less than the revelation of the glory of Jesus. In the prayers of the Mass, we repeatedly make reference to the fact that Jesus reigns in glory in the kingdom of God forever. But the transfiguration reminds us that forever means not only the future, but also the present; that when we experience the mysterious glory of Jesus at Mass, it is our brief opportunity to sample what we will know eternally in the kingdom of heaven.

REFLECTION QUESTIONS

❶ How can an increased appreciation for the Old Testament lead me to a greater understanding of Jesus' life, ministry, and person?

❷ If I were Peter, James or John and bore witness to the Transfiguration, what might my reaction be? What if I were Moses or Elijah?

❸ What does it mean to understand the Transfiguration as a mystery? Does learning more about this event make it more or less mysterious?

The
Institution of
the Eucharist

· ·
"DO THIS IN REMEMBRANCE OF ME."

✝ To connect the Gospel mystery of Jesus' institution of the Eucharist at the Last Supper with the Mass we celebrate in our Churches today might seem elementary, but is worthy of reflection. As Samuel Johnson once wrote, "People need to be reminded more often than they need to be instructed." And so it is helpful to remind ourselves of the significance of Christ's institution of the sacrament of his Body and Blood on the night he was betrayed.

We know that as he sat at table with his disciples in the Upper Room, Jesus instituted the Eucharist. At the same time, however, he also instituted the ministerial priesthood. The words of consecration of the bread and wine were followed by the instruction that the Apostles were to do what Jesus had just done in proclaiming that these elements were now his body, a command which meant that they too were now consecrated as the charter members of the Christian priesthood.

It is impossible to separate the Eucharist from the priesthood. Saint John Vianney, in his *Catechism on the Priesthood*, emphasizes this connection and also the centrality of these interlocking mysteries:

"When people wish to destroy religion, they begin by attacking the priest, because where there is no longer any priest there is no sacrifice, and where there is no longer any sacrifice there is no religion."

There have been some schools of thought in modernist Catholic circles which argue that anyone can and should be allowed to confect the Eucharist, that anyone can and should be able to boldly approach the altar of sacrifice, and that we should eliminate any disparity between the baptismal priesthood with which all Catholics are invested and the ministerial priesthood with which the clergy are specially invested. But if we reflect critically upon the life of Christ, we see that it was not while addressing the crowds that Jesus chose to institute the Eucharist, but in the exclusive company of the disciples whom he had hand picked. The priests from whom we receive the sacraments today are, like the first Apostles, those whom Jesus has hand picked to pass on his Body and Blood to us in Communion. The role of the priest is similar to the role of the mother; not everyone can or should be one, and so we must give special honor to those who are.

Outside of the Catholic Church, there are many interpretations as to what took place in the Upper Room and the implications of that event. Some believe that Last Supper was a one-time experience between Jesus and the Apostles, and there is no need to revisit it liturgically. This is hard to swallow if one reads the book of Acts, wherein Christian communities gather frequently for "the breaking of bread" that was the early Church's term for celebrating the Eucharist.

Others contend that when Jesus instructed his hearers to re-enact what they were witnessing, he meant they should do so merely as a memorial service. Curiously, the majority of these groups, when they celebrate Communion, retain the first person present tense in their liturgy, using the phrase "This is my body" at the presentation of the communion elements. And though these groups might contend that the elements that they distribute are mere reminders of the Last Supper, the ministers of Communion often use the phrases "the body of Christ" and "the blood of Christ" when offering the bread and the cup to individual participants—terms that seem out of place for a mere memorial.

Saint Paul tells us that what Jesus instituted at the Last Supper is exactly what he said it was—the giving of himself, Body and Blood, in a sacramental way that was meant to be continued throughout the life of his Church: "The cup of blessing that we bless, is it not a sharing in the blood of Christ? The bread that we break, is it not a sharing in the body of Christ?" (1 Corinthians 10:16).

Other translations of this passage talk about a "participation in" or a "communion with" the blood of Christ. But ironically, perhaps the strongest translation of this passage from Paul comes from one of the looser modern Bible translations, *The Message:*

> *"When we drink the cup of blessing, aren't we taking into ourselves the blood, the very life, of Christ? And isn't it the same with the loaf of bread we break and eat? Don't we take into ourselves the body, the very life, of Christ? Because there is one loaf, our many-ness becomes one-ness—Christ doesn't become fragmented in us. Rather, we become unified in him. We don't reduce Christ to what we are; he raises us to what he is."*

The last sentence of this translation is an obvious embellishment by the translators, but it makes a point that is at the center of our Catholic faith: Jesus did not give us the Eucharist merely so that he could remain with us on our level, but so that he could draw us up into the greater reality in which he lives and reigns. The unique intersection of heaven and earth which occurs at the words of consecration is not only intended so that heaven can pay earth a visit, but so that we who experience this intersection of the temporal and the eternal can allow ourselves to be challenged—even disturbed—to worship God not as we prefer to worship him, but as he has ordained for us to worship him. And the most perfect act of worship that he has given us is Communion with his very self in the the Eucharist.

REFLECTION QUESTIONS

❶ Can a better understanding of the Eucharist help me to better understand the role of priests in the Church? If so, how?

❶ How can I explain the Catholic understanding of what happens at Communion to a non-Catholic?

❸ How can I respect the office of the ministerial priesthood so as to understand that the calling of the priest and the calling of the laity are two distinct and honorable calls?

$\mathcal{A}$ppendix 1

. . . .

PRAYERS FOR MEDITATING UPON THE MYSTERIES
OF THE ROSARY IN THE CONTEXT OF THE MASS

✝ For those who may, after reading preceding chapters, wish for a more compact way to practically contemplate the mysteries before Mass, I have here included a shorter set of prayers designed for use in personal prayer. The reader may choose to briefly meditate upon the prayers associated with the five mysteries assigned to whatever day of the week he or she happens to be at Mass, or if arriving early enough before the beginning of the liturgy, quietly reflect on all twenty mysteries while waiting for Mass to begin. Of course, as mentioned in the preface, part of the joy of "riffing" on the rosary is developing one's own personalized method of entering more deeply into the events of the life of Christ.

· · · · · · · · · · · · · · · · · · ·
THE JOYFUL MYSTERIES

The Annunciation

Lord Jesus, as the Word of God, you were made flesh in the womb of Mary at the annunciation. Grant me the grace to recognize you in the bread and wine that will soon be made flesh upon the altar in the sacrament of the Eucharist.

The Visitation

Lord Jesus, Elizabeth greeted you with great joy when she encountered you in the womb of your mother, Mary. Grant me the grace to greet you with joy as I receive you in Holy Communion.

The Nativity

Lord Jesus, you gathered those of both humble and high estate to witness your birth into the world. Grant me the grace to recognize that I encounter you in the Mass not only as an individual, but also surrounded by your people from all walks of life.

The Presentation at the Temple

Lord Jesus, Simeon and Anna waited with expectant hope to greet you when you were presented at the Temple. Grant me the grace to wait for you eagerly as they did and to reflect their spirit of gratitude at having encountered you so intimately in the Eucharist.

The Finding in the Temple

Lord Jesus, your Father's house was the place in which your parents found you after much searching. Grant me the grace of understanding how I can know you in many settings but most perfectly in your Temple, where you dwell in sacrament.

. . . .
THE SORROWFUL MYSTERIES

The Agony in the Garden

Lord Jesus, you instructed your Apostles to watch and pray as you prepared to offer yourself in sacrifice. Grant me the grace to be attentive and reverent as I remember your sacrifice in the liturgy of Mass.

The Scourging at the Pillar

Lord Jesus, you present yourself to us in the Eucharist as an unbloody sacrifice. Grant me the grace to remember the sacrifice of which I partake at Communion is in fact one that required a great deal of blood from you. May my understanding of your suffering draw me into greater appreciation of your love for me.

The Crowning With Thorns

Lord Jesus, you were crowned by the soldiers not with the sovereignty which you deserved, but with mockery and derision. Grant me the grace to give thought of your sovereignty over all other thoughts as I prepare to receive you in Holy Communion.

The Carrying of the Cross

Lord Jesus, I know that the weights which I carry with me to Mass pale in comparison with the weight of the world which you carried on your shoulders to Calvary. Grant me the grace to follow the witness of Simon of Cyrene, who learned to recieve the cross with joy rather than reluctance.

The Crucifixion

Lord Jesus, in the Eucharist, we proclaim your death until you come again in glory. Grant me the grace to more perfectly appreciate your paschal sacrifice and gaze upon your crucified body not with horror, but with love.

. . . .
THE GLORIOUS MYSTERIES

The Resurrection

Lord Jesus, may your Body bring me to everlasting life as I receive your sacrament. Grant me the grace to desire a holy death so as to share in eternal life with you at my own resurrection.

The Ascension

Lord Jesus, from your seat at the right hand of the Father, you receive our prayers. Grant me the grace to receive you worthily now so as to be worthily received by you in your kingdom, where you live and reign forever.

The Descent of the Holy Spirit at Pentecost

Lord Jesus, you sent your Holy Spirit to empower your Apostles. Grant me the grace of seeing your Holy Spirit at work in the consecration of the elements of the altar and at work in the hands of the priests whom you have uniquely sent your Holy Spirit to make you present in sacrament.

The Assumption of Mary

Lord Jesus, your mother was set apart in holiness, and yet, because she was human as we are, she gives us hope that we can, like her, live with you in your kingdom forever. Grant me the grace to witness the Eucharistic mystery with Mary by my side so as to join her at your side in heaven.

The Coronation of Mary

Lord Jesus, Mary's blood ties to your royal person give her unique honor in the kingdom of God. Grant me the grace to understand that through baptism, I have also become a member of your family, and that worthily receiving Communion with your entire family gives me an inheritance in your kingdom alongside your Holy Mother.

. . . .
THE LUMINOUS MYSTERIES

The Baptism in the Jordan

Lord Jesus, you had no sin, and so your baptism was not one of repentance, but rather one of identification with our humanity. Grant me the grace of seeing my baptism as my membership in your family and participation in Holy Communion as my necessary maintenance of our family relationship.

The Wedding at Cana

Lord Jesus, at Cana you transformed water into wine. Grant me the grace to perceive the less visible sign of your transformation of wine into your own blood in the sacrament of the Eucharist.

The Proclamation of the Kingdom of God

Lord Jesus, you tell us that your kingdom is not of this world, and yet you have given us a foretaste of your kingdom in the Church which you have established for us. Grant me the grace to ever be humbly subject to the sacraments and their guardians which you have appointed for my salvation.

The Transfiguration

Lord Jesus, all of salvation history points to you as its glorious fulfillment. Grant me the grace of being attentive during the Liturgy of the Word to the ways in which your plan to give yourself to us in the Eucharist was taking shape even in the Old Testament.

The Institution of the Eucharist

Lord Jesus, you gave a hand-selected group of your followers a unique and specific way of sustaining your sacramental presence among us, especially in the Eucharist. Grant me the grace of giving you special honor in this sacrament, as well as special honor to those who you have called to be its guardians, your priests.

$\mathcal{A}ppendix\ 2$

PRAYING THE ROSARY AS A NEW CATHOLIC

✝ For many who have recently come into the Catholic faith, the immediate objection to praying something like the rosary comes from a learned repugnance toward the idea of "repetitious" prayer. Perhaps too many of us have seen Monty Python-esque film depictions of zombie-monks smacking themselves on the forehead after mindlessly repeating what appear to us to be arbitrary Latin phrases. However, looking at repetitious prayers through the eyes of authentic Catholic tradition renders them anything but impersonal.

All of us have experienced "dryness" in prayer; some have even experienced what Saint John of the Cross referred to as the "Dark Night of the Soul," wherein the most valiant efforts of ours to emotionally connect with God seem to be thwarted at every turn. For myself, as a potential Catholic first encountering the rosary, I had to get something of a running start to get over this hump of resistance to repetitive prayer. Being somewhat vaguely enamored with Catholicism in the days immediately preceding my conversion, I initially viewed praying of the rosary not as an indispensable tool for connecting me with the mysteries of the Gospel, but as a way to develop Catholic street credibility. At first, my enthusiasm for the rosary was borne more of a desire for social rather than spiritual inclusion in the Church. As an outsider looking hopefully in, I at first put the rosary in the same category as bingo and fish consumption on Fridays, viewing it as more of a way to culturally identify with other Catholics rather than a way to become caught up into the mysteries of the Gospel.

One of the main arguments made by non-Catholic Christians against the numerous repetitions of the Our Father, Hail Mary, and Glory Be contained in the rosary is that they violate Jesus' teaching against the piling up of "empty phrases" that he forbids in Matthew 6:7. And yet, as someone who has over the years come to deeply appreciate liturgy and devotion within the Catholic faith, I have become able, despite my strongest "protestant" impulses, to focus far more intently on my prayer intentions via these memorized offerings than I was ever able to in the spontaneous spiritual free-for-all sessions with God that I used to have before becoming Catholic.

Even as a non-Catholic Christian, I remember having trouble focusing during prayer. I would follow the occasional advice of certain pastors to write down a list of recurring prayer requests (a practice in which I still engage) so that I could reflect upon them in my regular prayer times. Ironically, despite my inherent distaste for repetitive Catholic prayers such as the rosary, I eventually came to understand that mechanically repeating a prayer request list at an arranged time was no different than what I perceived to be the mindless rattling off of the Our Father and Hail Mary that Catholics engaged in whenever they prayed the rosary. As I now know, discipline is integral to the Christian life, and sometimes that discipline takes shape in the form of repeated prayers.

When I attempt to pray, my human tendency is usually to do so in the form of spontaneous and unscripted prayer. Hence, a typical prayer progression for me might consist of praying for a person I know, moving on to the egregious and offensive faults of theirs for which I am praying, meditating upon those faults, remembering why it is their sin bugs me so much, and concluding by preparing in pensive detail how I myself plan to tell off the party in question if ever God grants me the opportunity to bring about his justice myself. By the end of this kind of prayer, I usually realize that I haven't been praying at all—I know that God has heard my reflection upon the matters important to me, but truth be told, when I pray in this way, I am more focused on my own ideas of justice and mercy than his.

As Catholics, our theology of prayer compels us to understand that the repeating of memorized phrases is intended to yank us outside of ourselves, which one might say ranks among the ultimate goals of Catholicism. I have to remind myself that Catholics are admonished by the Church to start our prayers of the rosary with a Hail Mary, not a "Hail Matt." We are called to pray the rosary in the name of the Father, Son, and Holy Spirit, not in the name of Me, Myself, and I. And as such, we must discipline ourselves to resolutely focus on the will of the Father for ourselves and our fellow persons, despite our pressing situations. Holy Mother Church tells us that there is no better way to do so than by meditation upon a memorized prayer, as many times as necessary, until the mind becomes conditioned to focus upon God and not upon ourselves. The greatest medicine the Church offers as a salve for the distracted mind is the rosary.

Some might suggest that the rosary is "old-school," an antiquated relic of days gone by; that it hearkens back to the preferences and tendencies of Catholic grandparents at the expense of alienating Catholic grandchildren. To such objectors, I ask: Is it really necessary for devotional practices to re-invent themselves with every successive generation? Why is it that whenever we find our own tendencies in disharmony with the Church, we so often demand that it be the Church that does the changing? As Catholics, can we reasonably maintain that God has changed his mind as to how we should approach him just because we may have changed our minds about how we prefer to approach him? Can we really assert that the wisdom of human progress is greater than the so-called "antiquated" wisdom of time-tested Catholic devotional practice?

As Catholics, we can (perhaps to clamorous disagreement from Christians from other sects) trace our foundation to Christ himself. On a daily basis, a number of non-Catholic admirers and followers of Jesus (as well as this Catholic author) frequently offer unscripted and quite valid prayers to him while remaining within the general Christian prayer tradition. But as Catholics, our sword for cutting through the battle lines of spiritual warfare is double-edged; we can pray spontaneously and in an unscripted fashion, but we can also offer memorized prayers to God from within our tradition. And that practiced tradition contains not only short memorized personal prayers such as the Our Father, but also communal devotion to the greatest memorized prayer of the Church, the commemoration of the true presence of Christ's Body and Blood at Mass. It is no mere memorial, nor is it a mere symbol; to view the Eucharist as such is to take a protestant interpretation of the sacrament.

Additionally, the use of memorized prayer should be neither new nor shocking in the longview of Christian tradition, and as such, devotion to it should be no surprise to non-Catholic Christian detractors who maintain that Catholic theology was an off-the-cuff invention of a fourth-century Constantinian regime.

To deny that Jesus ever intended to institute a religion requires an unprecedented suspension of disbelief. Who founds a business, hands a successor the keys to the building, and says, "Do whatever you like; just don't burn the place down"? There are protocols that every organization puts in place in their daily operations, not as obstacles, but rather as aids to efficiency. Such is the nature of the Church when she recommends to us the efficiency and effectiveness of the rosary.

Finally, it is helpful to reflect upon what is meant by "meditation" in the context of Catholic tradition. In my pre-Catholic days, I associated the general idea of meditation with Asian monks who prayed and squinted with all their might in the hopes of levitation in this life and nirvana in the next. Anyone who studies Eastern mystical theology knows that the eschatological hope of the Eastern mystic is to lose him or herself entirely, to disappear, as it is sometimes said, like a drop of rain might disappear in the ocean.

I have spoken with a few people who have been on Eastern-style spiritual retreats in the Buddhist and Hindu traditions.

I remember a conversation with one of these retreatants, who shared that the entire first day of one of his retreat experiences was focused on breathing exercises, and that the goal of the first twenty-four hours was for guests to focus on the difference between inhalation and exhalation, to try to meditate upon the millisecond in time when breathing in stopped and breathing out started.

As a casual observer of the phenomenon, it seems odd to me that materialist culture is so abstractly fascinated with Eastern spirituality, which upholds annihilation of the self as the goal of its eschatology. In light of the view of Eastern spirituality which seems to inform so many celebrity adherents, one might summarize this way of looking at the world by describing it as an ethos of "get all you can now, because tomorrow, you will be an indistinguishable piece of oblivion." When I hear pundits, actors, and athletes talk about the fact that they are not "religious" but "spiritual" people, I often wonder if they have thought through to the logical conclusions of such a position, namely the ultimate renunciation of self. I also wonder, at times jealously, how I might sign up for such a religion, which seems to demand almost nothing from its followers save for an amiable fondness?

When our meditation is focused on the inner workings of ourselves, why should we be surprised if we begin to worship the god upon whom we have been meditating, namely ourselves? If my bodily processes are what occupy my meditation, at some point, I am going to assign ultimate devotional importance to these bodily processes. As has been stated before in this volume, *lex orandi, lex credendi*—the law of prayer is the law of belief. The way I express myself devotionally shapes the way that I end up believing about reality. And the thing on which I meditate must eventually become my God.

Rather than focusing our thoughts inwardly, Catholic devotion is all about focusing on that which is outside of us. One of the most jarring and productive forms of this is the rosary. Even many protestant Christians, myself formerly among them, will admit that their unscripted prayer times often end up being primarily petitionary in nature, and that at the end of one's prayers, God has been given an awful lot of directives, while the person giving these directives has done very little in the way of asking what divine directives he or she needs to take away from the conversation.

Catholic meditation, in contrast to nearly every other form of spiritual meditation, requires us to focus upon things outside of ourselves rather than things within us so that the benefits can be given back to us in a way that is meaningful not only to us but to all Christians. The Assumption of Mary is a perfect example. As Catholics, praying this mystery requires us to focus on the holiness of someone outside of ourselves, which, incidentally, requires us to admit that we are not the only persons on this earth with any kind of claim to holiness, and additionally, that no matter the claims we make to holiness, someone has a greater claim to it than we do. If Mary has been assumed and we haven't, then there is work to be done on our part. Also, if we rightly subscribe to the theology that Mary was assumed *body and soul* into heaven, then all hopes of being eventually dissolved and annihilated into the ether are out of the question—our body and souls are destined, as are the body and soul of Mary, to persist. We will, as some have said, be more ourselves in heaven than we are here on earth. Catholic prayer, especially the rosary, helps us to hone our meditative perspective not on the annoyances and aspirations of our lives which might otherwise "slow down the server" with our machine-gun petitions, but rather calls us to stretch the focus of our prayer outside of our own experience and into the experience of Christ and even that of his Mother.

Last of all, I feel the need to dispel any myths that the rosary is meant to be some sort of "lucky charm" that Catholics carry around so that they won't be hit by cars or so their plane won't crash. The rosary is perhaps anything *but* such a talisman. The rosary is not a mere security blanket, fashion accessory, or Catholic identification card; it is instead one of the most important aids to Catholic prayer. There are some who objectify the rosary by wearing it in the same way that some non-practicing Christians often wear crucifixes: because it's pretty, functions as a good accessory, and vaguely refers to a worldview the wearer isn't completely hostile toward. With all these potential benefits and so few repercussions, why not keep a rosary or two in the wardrobe?

On the contrary, as it has been stated earlier in this book, the rosary is not a self-sustaining device but a way of prayer. One might accurately state that wearing a rosary comes close to being a useless practice if praying the rosary is not a part of the life of the wearer. It is not as though God checks pockets at the gate of heaven to see who has a rosary or who doesn't before letting people in. Knowing all, seeing all, and hearing all, our Almighty Father understands who carries a rosary out of a desire to connect with him on a deeper level and who carries one because it looks good with a certain belt.

The reasons for carrying the rosary on our persons should be neither fashion nor mere identification. If we go to the trouble to throw a rosary in our pockets along with our keys when we go in to work, it should be because we have at least the slimmest intention of praying a line or two of it before we arrive home that evening.

Sources

Constitution on the Sacred Liturgy (*Sacrosanctum Concilium*), Second
  Vatican Council (regarding "active participation"). December 4,
  1963. Available at www.vatican.va.

English translation of *Catechism of the Catholic Church for the United States
  of America*, copyright © 1994, United States Catholic Conference,
  Inc.—Libreria Editrice Vaticana.

Dolan, Timothy. "Priests for the Third Millenium," *Our Sunday Visi-
  tor*. September 1, 2000 (quoting Pope John XXIII).

Lewis, C. S. *Letters to Malcolm: Chiefly on Prayer*. Harvest Books, 2002.
  Copyright © 1964, 1963 by C. S. Lewis PTE Limited, Copyright
  renewed 1992, 1991 by Arthur Owen Barfield.

———.*Mere Christianity*. HarperOne, 2001. Copyright © C. S. Lewis
  Pte. Ltd. 1942, 1943, 1944, 1952.

Liguori, Saint Alphonsus. *Way of the Cross: St. Alphonsus Liguori*. Liguori Publications, 1994. Copyright © 1983 and 1994, Liguori
  Publications.

Pope Benedict XVI. Post-Synodal Apostolic Exhortation on the
  Eucharist as the Source and Summit of the Church's Life and
  Mission (*Sacramentum Caritatis*). February 22, 2007. Available at
  www.vatican.va.

*The Princess Bride: S. Morgenstern's Classic Tale of True Love and High Ad-
  venture*, abridged by William Goldman. Harcourt, 2007. Copyright
  © 1973, 1998, 2003 by William Goldman.

Vianney, Saint John. *Catechism on the Priesthood*.